PARTICIPATORY COMMUNITY DEVELOPMENT APPROACH

TRAINING MANUAL

Published By

Dr. Agnes N. Masika 1st Edition

ISBN 978-9914-9930-0-4

DEDICATION

To the body of Jesus Christ

"But also, for this very reason, giving all diligence, add to your faith virtue, to virtue knowledge,

to knowledge self-control, to self-control perseverance, to perseverance godliness, to godliness brotherly kindness,

and to brotherly kindness love"

(2 Peter 1:5-7)

(NKJV)

TABLE OF CONTENTS

FOREWORD

Dr. Agnes Masika is a renowned development worker who has done a lot of work in this area of Community Participatory Development with the goal of improving the lives of grassroots communities.

In this manual she has outlined Participatory Community Development Methodologies which will enable communities to be in charge of the kind of development they need. These approaches give communities an opportunity to express and analyze their situation, to prioritize their needs, and plan for what action should be taken to remedy their problems. She has in this manual ably described community concepts, community organization, community situation analysis, community action planning, project management and resource mobilization. She has in the last section dealt with the components of project proposal writing which is key to resource mobilization and fundraising for development projects. The manual is useful reference material for communities, project planners, project implementers, proposal writers for fundraising, researchers, teachers, students, and all other stakeholders of Participatory Community Development.

All stakeholders are therefore encouraged to make maximum use of this Participatory Community Development Approach Training Manual, in order to appropriately delve into community development approaches for improvement of communities' wellbeing.

DR. BENARD NAMUSASI CHINUNGO
CEO, Capacity and Training Institute
Email: bnamusasi@gmail.com

ACKNOWLEDGEMENTS

The motivation to write this participatory Community Development Approach Training Manual was the desire to consolidate my experiences of working with communities using participatory approach over twenty years and share with other stakeholders in the area of Community Development and Project Development and Management. I therefore sincerely thank Dr. Benard Namusasi Chinungo, CEO, Capacity and Training Institute, for writing the Forward.

Dr. Namusasi has passion for community empowerment and a champion of Competency Based Training for imparting knowledge, skills and aptitude to fulfill the required Occupational Standards for community service. With his famous slogan of "Yesu Rohoni and Pesa Mfukoni" (Translated "Jesus in our hearts, Money in our pockets") he believes, this training manual can help impart the necessary competences to Church Ministers in accordance to Occupational Standards to effectively serve the community and empower them spiritually, socially and economically.

He recommends the manual as a useful reference material to stakeholders with an agenda of community development. I am greatly indebted to him Prof. Kukubo Barasa, a renowned Educationist and author of over 20 books particularly in the area of Adult Education. He has been a Senior Lecturer at the University of Nairobi and Kenyatta University for over 30 years. He is currently a Director at Capacity and Training Institute. He is a strong believer and Champion of Second Chance Opportunity Training and Skills Development to all people without any discrimination whatsoever.

He has passion to develop higher capacity for learning at any stage of life, as it is never too late to learn something new.

He played the role of Quality Assurance by editing and proof reading to ensure the book meets the highest professional and educational standards. I am greatly indebted to him.

My gratitude to Lucy Kavila of Government Press, Kenya. She ensured the book is professionally printed to the highest standards. I am greatly indebted to her.

My family who endured my long hours at the desk as I put the book together. I thank you very much for your understanding, patience and perseverance for a fine outcome of the book that will positively impact on many users for transformational change in their lives and the community in general.

Many thanks to you all.

May God abundantly bless you.

DR. AGNES N. MASIKA,
Email: agmasika07@gmail.com.

INTRODUCTION

Participatory approaches are effective tools for causing development by the people for the people. These approaches are empowering processes that will enable people to make informed choices and decisions based on collective analysis. The more involved or consulted people are, the greater will be their commitment in the implementation and sustenance of the project at hand.

Mwalimu Julius Nyerere, the first President of the Republic of Tanzania aptly said, "people will only develop themselves by what they do: they develop themselves by making their own decisions, by increasing their own full participation as equals." Participatory Community Development is therefore a process through which community can influence, share and control development initiatives and resources and make informed decisions for the purposes of ownership and sustainability of those initiatives.

In this regard, participatory approaches allow communities to express and analyze the realities of their lives, plan themselves what action to take to change the situation, monitor and evaluate results and also share whatever accruing benefits or losses. Participatory community development enables communities or groups of people to strive to make it possible for all of its members to satisfy their fundamental human needs and enhance the quality of their lives.

The purpose of this training manual is therefore to introduce participatory methodologies to planning which can be used to build and empower communities to formulate and implement their community development projects.

The manual is designed for use by trainers who will work with communities and other development agents to help them analyze, prioritize, strategize plans and implement community-based programs. The manual will be the basis of training consisting of modules that can be used to plan and organize workshops for capacity building and empowering a participatory development planning.

The book includes:

Module 1: Community Development Concepts
Module 2: Community Organization
Module 3: Community Situation Analysis
Module 4: Community Strategic and Action Planning
Module 5 Project Planning and Management
Module 6: Resource Mobilization for Project Implementation.

MODULE 1

COMMUNITY DEVELOPMENTS CONCEPTS

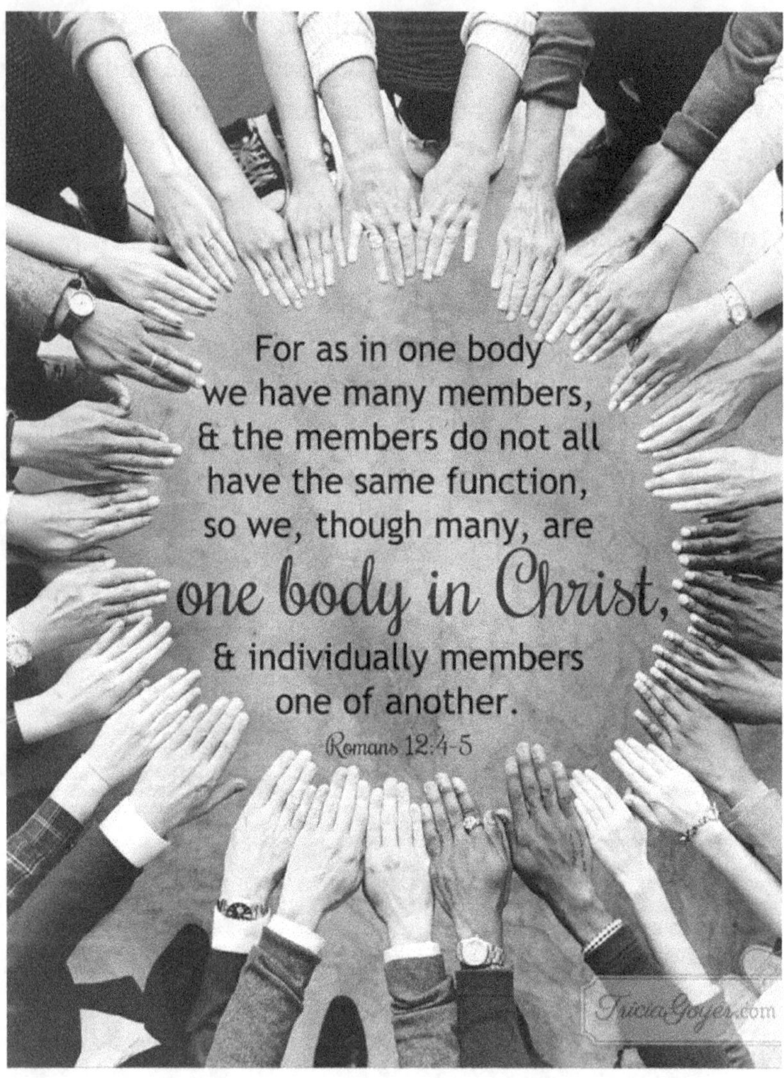

1.1 Introduction

This module explains concepts used in the community development context. It aims at creating a common understanding among community development practitioners.

1.2 Objectives

By the end of this module the participants will be able to:

1. Define:
   - □ Community
   - □ Development
   - □ Sustainable development
   - □ Participation
   - □ Mobilization

2. Describe how to mobilize community for participation in community projects.

3. Explain barriers to community mobilization.

4. Describe different forms of community participation and barriers to community participation.

1.3 Definitions of Concepts

1.3.1 Community

The idea of community comes from the sense of responsibility we have for each other. According to the scriptures, God encourages us to take care of our brothers and sisters - whether friends or enemies!

Now I plead with you, brethren, by the name of our Lord Jesus Christ, that you all speak the same thing, and that there be no divisions among you, but that you be perfectly joined together in the same mind and in the same judgment. 1Corithians 1: 10 (NKJV)

Definition of the term Community

A community is a group of people in the same geographical area who share a common culture or similar traditions, customs, way of living and share the same social facilities.

The Church describes the Church as a community, as a people. of God. Further it declares that this community is a primary object of God's plan for salvation, a great example of this was the early church of Acts, which made a habit of meeting together, eating together, and worshiping together. As a result, ***"the Lord added to their number daily those who were being saved" (Acts 2:46–47 NKJV).***

The church ministers and Community Development Practitioners should understand the community by knowing what will make it acceptable at individual and community levels.

Exercise: Meaning of a Face.

1. When you look at a person, especially one among the community, would you say that you understand the person behind the expression?

Would you then generalize about that particular community or make stereotyped comments about communities? e.g.

- ☐ That community is lazy.
- ☐ They are a bunch of thieves; they steal everything on sight.
- ☐ They are all cattle rustlers.
- ☐ They are too backwards to comprehend anything.

John 7:24 (NKJV), "Do not judge according to appearance, but judge with righteous judgment."

Acts 10: 34-35(NIV), "So Peter opened his mouth and said: "Truly I understand that God shows no partiality, but in every nation anyone who fears him and does what is right is acceptable to him."

2. Look at the picture of a face below:

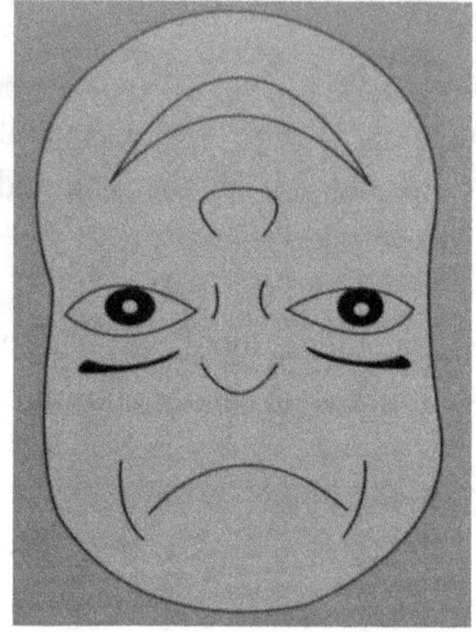

(a) Describe what you see in the drawing.

Response should include.

Sad face, angry look, gloomy face, unhappy man, disgruntled fellow:

(b) Now turn the picture upside down and describe what you see.

(c) Relate the illustration to community development.

Individuals and communities cannot and should not be taken for granted or at facial appearance. Therefore, it is essential to;

1. Understand each member as a person as regards to:
    - Individuals interests, strengths, weaknesses, experiences and levels of mobilization.
    - Individual's personal beliefs, values, perceptions, peer inhabitants, and aspirations or hopes for self- development and attitudes

2. Recognize social-cultural realities:
   - ☐ Groups decision making procedures.
   - ☐ Traditional values and norms
   - ☐ Gender and age group relationships
   - ☐ Communication patterns.
3. Be involved in the life of the community by:
   - ☐ Mixing with the groups and participating in their activities so as to gain acceptance and to identify with their interests.
   - ☐ Making friends with members – visiting and being visited (beware of exploiting and being exploited)
   - ☐ Attending functions such as weddings rituals, funerals
   - ☐ Interviewing or talking to willing contacts, community leaders, traders, chiefs, market women to gain better understanding of their worries, hopes, problems and expectations.
   - ☐ Identifying opinion leaders and innovators who are likely to influence others.

1.3.2 Development

"And whatever you do, do it heartily as to the Lord and not to men. Knowing that from the Lord you will receive the reward of inheritance for you serve the Lord Christ but he who does wrong will be repaid for what he has done and there is no partiality." Colossians 3:23-25 (NKJV)

CASE STUDY

Wata Constituency

Mr. Lowi had been the area Member of Parliament for 20 years during the one party era. During this period, no development took place, all the infrastructure was in a dilapidated state. The roads had huge craters and motorists found it safer to drive on the footpaths, endangering the lives of pedestrians. The bridges were made of wooden poles, threatening to carve in under the pressure of vehicles. Occasionally the community would repair the bridges by putting stones and sand.

The roads became completely impassable during the rainy season. The school buildings did not have windows and doors. The pupils took their lessons while sitting on bare dusty floors except for a few innovative pupils who made stools for themselves out of stones or wood. Most schools had only six teachers for the whole primary school. Out of which only one was a trained teacher. The staff room was a small wooden structure, barely furnished. The dispensary was also made of wooden structure, with one enrolled nurse to serve a population of 5000 people.

Occasionally, religious organizations would organize to bring on board qualified medical personnel who would also come with medical supplies. About fifty percent of school going children were at home helping their parents with domestic chores. Their parents could not afford the high school levies. Ninety percent of the people were living in abject poverty.
At the advent of the multiparty era, Mr. Lowi was declared obsolete and voted out. Mr. Kasi, a visionary and people centered leader was elected MP with landslide victory. Within three months in office, he embarked on a community initiative development agenda. He constructed constituency office where weekly community meetings were held to discuss and chart the development course of the area. Development committees were formed and charged with the responsibility of ensuring the projects are implemented as scheduled. Review of progress of development projects was done on monthly basis to ensure everything was on course.

Any corrective measures needed were done promptly by the responsibilities committees. Mr. Kasi encouraged the community to contribute ideas, materials and whatever finances they could afford towards the development of the agenda of the area. He actively sourced for funds from the government and development partners to supplement community contribution for the development of the constituency.

It is now four years down the line and the change in development of the area is tremendous. The roads are now all weather with strong bridges. New schools have been built, including staff rooms and staff quarters are well equipped and furnished.

The dispensary is also new, adequately staffed with qualified personnel including highly qualified medical volunteers from friendly development partners. High quality medical supplies are promptly received on a monthly basis. The bursary fund has enabled many children to enroll in schools. Mr. Kasi is in the process of initiating a micro-finance project that is aimed at empowering people economically.

Discussion

Share your experiences of leadership and development in your area for the last ten years.

Definition of the term Development

Development is the process of expanding and improving social infrastructure such as education, health, food security, social welfare as the environment is safe guarded with the aim of improving people's quality of life and also contributing to the growth of the national economy.

Exercise

Discuss what the development efforts are in your area e.g.

(a) What is the status of infrastructure in your area?

(b) What is the status of the environment?

(c) What economic issues does the community experience?

1.3.3 Sustainable Development

Jeremiah 2:7 (NKJV), "I brought you into a bountiful country, to eat its fruit and its goodness. But when you entered, you defiled My Land and made My heritage an abomination."

CASE STUDY: Joy's Village

Joy nostalgically remembers her life as a young girl growing up in the village. She was adventurous and courageous. She would accompany her brothers to look after their father's livestock in the nearby fields. The pastures were green and in plenty with many indigenous trees including wild fruit trees. These trees were home for many birds hoping from branch to branch singing melodious songs.

Her brothers would tell her the names of different fruits as they picked fruits from different trees for a feast. They would also tell her names of different birds and explain to her the lifestyles of each bird species. The river was big; its water was clean with a variety of aquatic lives. When they took the animals for watering, they too would take a good swim and later bask on the nearby rocks. In the evening as she headed home, she would carry a bundle of firewood for her mother.

Today whenever Joy is on leave and traces her footsteps back to the village up to the grazing fields, she is amazed at the state of the environment of her former Garden of Eden. The grazing fields are brown with hardly any vegetation. The huge indigenous trees are all gone; the wild fruits and melodious songs from the birds are all no more. The river is all brown and has been reduced to a seasonal stream. The herdsmen have to queue to water their animals in turns and the diminished water resources have become a constant cause of herdsmen's conflicts.

Discussion:

1. What kind of environment did Joy grow up in?
2. Describe the changes that occurred in the environment.
3. What are the long-term effects of these environmental changes?

Definition of the term Sustainable Development

Sustainable development is development which meets the needs of the present generation, without compromising the ability of future generations to meet their own needs using the same resources.

- Discuss the kind of development that has taken place in Joy's Village?

Exercise

(a) Discuss the conditions of these resources listed below in the area you came from.

1. Vegetation.
2. Land
3. Water Resources
4. Environment

(b) What will be the condition of these resources in the next ten years from now?

(c) What can be done to rectify the situation?

1.3.4. Participation

Romans 12 3: "For by the grace given me I say to every one of you: Do not think of yourself more highly than you ought, but rather think of yourself with sober judgment, in accordance with the faith God has distributed to each of you. For just as each of us has one body with many members, and these members do not all have the same function, so in Christ we, though many, form one body, and each member belongs to all the others. We have different gifts, according to the grace given to each of us. If your gift is prophesying, then prophesy in accordance with your faith; if it is serving, then serve; if it is teaching, then teach; if it is to encourage, then give encouragement; if it is giving, then give generously; if it is to lead, do it diligently; if it is to show mercy, do it cheerfully Love must be sincere. Hate what is evil; cling to what is good. Be devoted to one another in love. Honor one another above yourselves Never be lacking in zeal, but keep your spiritual fervor, serving the Lord. Be joyful in hope, patient in affliction, faithful in prayer. Share with the Lord's people who are in need. Practice hospitality.

CASE STUDY: Southeast Province Development Status

After ten years of an international NGO involvement in development among the communities, a report prepared by external consultants showed that the NGO had failed to mobilize communities to actively participate in sustainable development of the area. In fact, the report indicated that instead of the communities had become parasites on the NGO and were unable to initiate, plan and their own projects.

A highly placed officer of the government was invited to comment on the report which was strongly worded stating, "these NGO people have completely disabled the communities. They have turned them into beggars, their development is not sustainable at all; they have created white elephants all over the place; the earth dams, the access roads, the school feeding programs, the highly subsidized income generating projects. After the NGO phases out all these projects will simply collapse!" In the context of these two reports, the government official had no doubt as to the level of the community's participation in the development process and was quite disturbed. You as a community worker with the NGO have the same sentiments as the officer and believe with all your heart that community participation is the answer to sustainable development.

Exercise

Discuss what made it difficult for the communities to participate in the community project (think about the situation in your own region)

What lessons can be learnt from what you have discussed from the scripture above the case study?

Definition of the term Participation

Response should include: -

Participation is when the community is actively involved in the development process, i.e., the community is actively involved in the problem identification, prioritization, planning, implementation, monitoring and evaluation using available resources. Participation allows communities to give feedback on project successes and failures and the reason for them and propose corrective measures.

1.3.4.1 Different forms of Participation

Different forms of participation are consultation participation, contribution participation, control participation, and passive participation.

(i) Consultation Participation

This is about involving the beneficiaries in gathering information concerning the project and also giving their views about it.

(ii) Contribution Participation

Beneficiaries also give ideas and items for the project implementation in material form e.g., sand, stones, timber, labour, money/ funds.

Contribution participation also include:

- Establishing of beneficiary management committees
- Beneficiaries having a role in maintenance of project activities.
- Involving the beneficiaries in project monitoring and evaluation

(iii) Control Participation

It is when beneficiaries make decisions, take responsibilities or are in charge during the project implementation. People should be responsible for their own affairs.

(iv) Passive Participation

Beneficiaries are told what is going to happen or has already happened. Announcements are made by authorities e.g. Government, NGOs, leaders, without listening or taking into account beneficiaries concerns or responses.

1.3.4.2 Barriers to Community Participation

Barriers to community participation include.

- Unclear policies/laws
- Participation driven by outsiders.
- Lack of transparency or openness
- Inappropriate use of government resources
- Poor community entry points
- Failure to respect community culture.
- Wrong timing
- Lack of motivation
- Failure of community members to respond to project advisors

1.3.5 Mobilization

Esther 4:16 (NKJV), "Go, gather all the Jews who are present in Shushan, and fast for me; neither eat nor drink for three days, night or day. My maids and I will fast likewise. And so I will go to the king, which is against the law; and if I perish, I perish!" Esther mobilized her Jewish people to fast and pray to save themselves from extermination.

Case Study: **Mwamba Village Water Project**

The people of Mwamba village were a worried lot. Their only river that transverses their area was drying up. There was hardly enough water for their domestic use and their livestock. Faced with this predicament the Village leader called a meeting for all members; men, women and the youth to discuss the issue and chart a way forward. After a long discussion it was resolved that the water from the river was adequate for livestock use only. Moreover, it was not fit for domestic use in its current state Therefore, a borehole was to be dug to provide water for domestic use.

However, the main obstacle to realization of this goal was lack of funds. It was unanimously agreed that every household will gives one head of cattle for sale to raise the funds required and the youth; male and female to provide the labor and also supervise and manage the construction of the borehole. They approached the Ministry of Water and Ministry of Works officials and a local NGO who agreed to give them the technical support. The borehole was successfully dug and all the people of Mwamba village enjoy their clean and fresh water from it and they even use some water from it for watering their kitchen gardens.

Discussion

1. What Made Village Mwamba Project Successful?
2. What Lessons Can Be Learnt from The Project?
3. What similarities are there with the verses given, Esther 4:46?

Definition of the term mobilization

Mobilization is recruiting or gathering people together in the community for a common purpose e.g.

(i) Social purpose – gather people to create awareness about a new idea or to contribute towards building community facilities like school, health center, water tank.

(ii) Political purpose: - gather people to encourage them to vote as a community block to have representation in position of leadership and authority.

(iii) Economic purpose- mobilize and organize community in groups e.g., chamas for income generating projects.

1.3.5.1 Steps in Community Mobilization

Steps to follow when mobilizing a community for a specific purpose include,

(i) Identify entry points to the community e.g.
- Community leaders
- Religious organizations
- Family gatherings
- Other social event

(ii) Develop the correct attitude. have positive attitude towards the community so as to empower them towards getting involved in their own affairs. refer to the picture of the face.

(iii) Identify community problems /needs and prioritize them. e.g., water, health, education, roads

(iv) Involve community resource personnel e.g.
- People who have shown leadership skills
- People with special skills and are charismatic.
- Opinion leaders

(v) Plan carefully what you intend to do with the community. Care should be taken when dealing with people's attitudes. Exercise patience and persistence because this process can be very slow.

1.3.5.2 Barriers to Community Mobilization

Some common barriers to community mobilization include

- Failure to identify correct entry points.
- Having wrong attitude
- Failure to identify community needs.
- Failure to involve community leaders.
- Poor or lack of planning on what you intend to do with the community.
- Impatience and lack of persistence
- Lack of resources, i.e., funds, treatment etc.
- Insecurity
- Ignorance

MODULE 2

COMMUNITY ORGANIZATION

2.1 Introduction

This module explains how to organize communities in groups through which development process can be facilitated. It also explains the importance of good leadership and effective communication as a way of enhancing the communities' abilities to achieve sustainable development. It also discusses group conflict and conflict resolution, negotiation, lobbying and team building for effective community participation.

I Corinthians 12:12-27 (NKJV). "For as the body is one and has many members, but all the members of that one body, being many, are one body, so also is Christ. For by one Spirit we were all baptized into one body—whether Jews or Greeks, whether slaves or free—and have all been made to drink into one Spirit.

For in fact the body is not one member but many. If the foot should say, "Because I am not a hand, I am not of the body," is it therefore not of the body? And if the ear should say, "Because I am not an eye, I am not of the body," is it therefore not of the body? If the whole body were an eye, where would be the hearing? If the whole were hearing, where would be the smelling?

But now God has set the members, each one of them, in the body just as He pleased. And if they were all one member, where would the body be? But now indeed there are many members, yet one body. And the eye cannot say to the hand, "I have no need of you";; nor again the head to the feet, "I have no need of you." No, much rather, those members of the body which seem to be weaker are necessary. And those members of the body which we think to be less honorable, on these we bestow greater honor; and our unpresentable parts have greater modesty, but our presentable parts have no need.

But God composed the body, having given greater honor to that part which lacks it, that there should be no schism in the body, but that the members should have the same care for one another. And if one member suffers, all the members suffer with it; or if one member is honored, all the members rejoice with it. Now you are the body of Christ, and members individually.

So is our community made of different people with their unique characters but we need each other as we are interdependent as much as we are independent individuals.

CASE STUDY: Mwamba Village Water Projects

Mwamba village water project was a success story narrated over and over again in every village gathering. As a result, people of Sandi Village decided to emulate the water project as they were also facing a water problem. A retired civil servant, Mr. Mustafa from the village volunteered to lead them to realize their dream. Mr. Mustafa convinced the village members that he will guide the implementation of the water project to completion within a very short time as he had a long experience in management of water projects.

When the village members agreed to make him the water project manager, he informed them that for ease of management and coordination of the project, his wife will be the treasurer, his sister the secretary, his elder son the youth leader. The village members were eager to have the water project completed and therefore they quickly contributed the money for implementation of the project. The money was banked in Mr. Mustafa's personal bank account.

It is now two years down the line and there is no sign of a water project. When the community members asked Mr. Mustafa why the project had not taken off, he said he was still waiting for the technical approval from the Ministry of Water. He cautioned them to stop bothering him with unnecessary questions as he was only volunteering to do the job for them.

In the meantime, Mr. Mustafa opened a shop and also bought a public service vehicle. The shop was managed by the wife and the vehicle driven by his son. The youth were so infuriated by the turn of events and they threatened to torch all his businesses unless a proper account of the project money was given.

Discuss

1. 1.Compare and contrast the management of Mwamba and Sandi water projects.
2. What can be done to solve the stalemate at Sandi water project?
3. What do we learn from 1 Corinthians 12:12-27 about community groups and projects?

2.2 Objectives

By the end of this module, you should be able to:

i. Define Community Group

- Describe stages of group development
- Discuss group conflicts and how they occur.
- Discuss conflict resolution.
- Negotiation
- Describe how to build group teams.
- Explain member's roles in team building.
- Networking
- Advocacy
- Lobbing

ii. Define leadership

- Describe qualities of a good leader.
- Describe leadership styles, their advantages and disadvantages.

iii. Define Communication

- Effective Communication
- Describe the Communication Process
- Explain the Purpose of Communication
- Discuss Communication Barriers
- Explain How to Overcome Barriers to Communication

2.3 Community Groups

Definition of a community group

A community group is a group of members, at least a minimum of five people, who have voluntarily come together with a spirit of cooperation to work together for a mutual social or economic benefit or to achieve common benefit or to achieve a common goal. These groups are initiated, managed and owned by the community members themselves.

2.3.1 Types of Community Groups

Community groups can either be formal or non-formal.

i. Formal groups

These are registered by government authorities and are governed by leadership structures, with binding constitution. They have a legal status e.g., registered women groups, youth groups, self- help groups and welfare societies.

ii. Non-Formal groups

These are unregistered groups with loose management structures usually guided by cultural values, common good. They have no legal status, e.g.

- Clan groups
- Traditional/cultural institutions

2.3.2. Benefits of Community Groups

Benefits of community groups include.

- When people form themselves into groups, they create opportunities for identifying and analyzing their needs and problems for better understanding of their situations, to find a lasting solution to their needs/problems.
- Group members can pull together limited resources which they can own and manage themselves in order to address community needs /problems such as poverty, food shortage, lack of water, poor health, illiteracy etc.
- Any projects developed by the group are owned by them. This gives group members a sense of ownership which is very important for success and sustainability of the projects.
- Community groups are built on cultural tradition of self-help, hence will be easy to mobilize and organize them.
- It is not easy to facilitate community development process through individuals. Groups are easily accessible by development partners. Stakeholders have easy access to goods and services and move faster in activities than on an individual basis.

- Community groups serve to empower the poor by giving them a platform for collective voice. They build power among themselves with which to confront the powerful economic /social and political forces, which are normally used to maintain the community in silence and poverty.

- Groups provide opportunities for members to talk matters over with those whom they intimately know and trust and therefore get the much-needed information for decision making.

2.3.3. How to Form Community Groups

Some ideas on how to facilitate communities to organize themselves into groups include.

Where there are no community groups it is important to facilitate the community to form themselves into groups, using the following procedures.

i. Explain to community members to understand and agree on the need to form a group to enable them achieve common goals and objectives.

ii. Allow membership to be open and voluntary for those who have attained the legal adult age.

iii. The group should not have political or religious interference.

iv. Make members aware or be informed about the personal skills and how to use them in solving the problems and their general needs.

v. Ask the group to choose leaders who will form the management committee, comprising.
    - Chairman,
    - Vice Chairperson,
    - Secretary,
    - Vice Secretary,
    - Treasurer,
    - Committee Members (number depends on the size of the group representing different members' interest e.g., gender, special skills, or expertise).

vi. Explain the roles and responsibilities of members of the management committee.

vii. Encourage the group to be registered by the relevant authorities to acquire legal status.

2.3.4 Stages of Group Development

When several people come together to work as a group on a project, they are not necessarily a productive team. Before a group of people can function well together, they must pass through a series of development stages, as explained below.

(i) Group Formation Stage

- People come together after identifying a common problem.
- Individuals want to establish personal identity and make an impression.
- Participation is limited as individuals get familiar with each other.
- Individuals begin to focus on tasks at hand and discuss its purpose.
- Members are essentially making ground rules on future decisions and actions will be based.

(ii) Storming Stage

- The group tries to deal with initial problems.
- These are lots of ultra-group conflicts.
- Individuals may become hostile towards each other and express their individuality by pursuing personal agenda.
- Friction increases, rules are broken, arguments occur.
- If successfully handled, this stage leads to new and relisting setting of objectives procedures and norms.

(iii) Norming Stage

- Characterized by overcoming tensions.
- Develop group cohesion in which norms are established and practiced.
- Group members accept the group.
- Group allegiance develops and members strive to maintain it.
- Members develop group spirit where harmony becomes important and group vision is further developed.

(iv) Performing Stage

- Characterized by mutual and maximum productivity.
- Develop mutual acceptance and membership.
- Members take on roles to fulfil the group's activities.
- Member's energy is channeled into identified tasks.
- New insights and solutions begin to emerge.
- Control and organization of work and activities also emerge.
- Members become willing to take significant risks.

Exercise

Discuss and identify particular stages of development in groups that you are interacting with. Give reason for the choice of the group development stage.

2.3.5 Factors that Can Influence Group Performance

Identified factors that can influence group performance include.

(i) Group Dynamics

These are forces that drive group performance. This should be powerful, productive and united.

- Emphasis in groups is on multidiscipline of members.by working as some group members can approach a situation from different perspectives, carefully monitor each other's work and carry out several tasks simultaneously.
- The performance and output of a group maybe greater than the sum of its individual members.

(ii) Group Norms

These are values that group members hold concerning acceptance behavior and create channel of interpersonal integration, the norms cover people, physical objects and value judgement. Norms become a guide for group behavior.

(iii) Group Cohesiveness

This is the amount of unity in the group. It is reflected in the attitude and action of group members. Members do things together and are mindful of each other.

2.3.6 Group Conflicts

Genesis 13:5-9 (NKJV) Lot also, who went with Abram, had flocks and herds and tents. Now the land was not able to support them, that they might dwell together, for their possessions were so great that they could not dwell together. And there was strife between the herdsmen of Abram's livestock and the herdsmen of Lot's livestock. The Canaanites and the Perizzites then dwelt in the land. So, Abram said to Lot, "Please let there be no strife between you and me, and between my herdsmen and your herdsmen; for we are brethren. Is not the whole land before you? Please separate from me. If you take the left, then I will go to the right; or, if you go to the right, then I will go to the left."

Analyze conflict between Abram and Lot

Define the term conflict.
Conflicts are disagreements between two or more individuals or groups. Or it is any tension affecting or causing differences between or among people resulting from perceived or real efforts, which interfere with the achievements of a goal by the other party. Sources of conflict within a group include:

- When people have little contact with each other and are dependent on one other for resources.
- When people or one member cannot perform a task until other member has completed the work
- When people/members reform a talk and then a decision is made as to which unit receives the output
- When members mutually interact in the exchange of resources
- When existing goal incompatibility e.g., increased security in stores due to theft may affect timely dispatch of goods/items between the store man and security officer.
- When scarce resources must be shared, rewarding system is inconsistent within a group.

2.3.6.1 Levels at which Conflicts Occur

Conflicts usually occur at three levels

(A) Personal level
(B) Interpersonal
(C) Group level

(a) Personal Level

The main source of conflicts at personal level is confusion over values, mental blockage (preventing one from thinking straight) and personal ego.

(b) Interpersonal Level

At interpersonal level, conflicts are caused by inadequate communication. threatened identity, threatened status, different value systems. assumptions and attitudes.

(c) Group Level

Group level conflicts are caused by insufficient communication, different value systems, different attitude and assumptions.

2.3.6.2 Symptoms of Unresolved Conflict

Common symptoms of unresolved conflicts are:

- Low interaction and sudden withdrawals
- Avoiding others
- Low morale coupled with poor performance and perpetual absentees.
- Poor interpersonal relationships manifesting as quarrels, backbiting, moody outbursts without reasonable cause.
- Expulsion of members from the group
- Faking peace by avoiding discussing issues.

2.3.6.3 Conflict Resolution

In resolving a conflict, there are three major goals:

(A) Lose-lose.
(B) Win-lose.
(C) Win-win

(a) Lose-lose.

Both parties lose where there is no compromise or taking of a middle ground in a dispute.

(b) Win-lose.

This is a situation when one party marshals its forces to win. It is characterized by parties directing their energies towards each other, looking at the issues at hand from their own point of view, and emphasizing on solutions rather than attainment of goals, values or objectives.

(c) Win-win

This is a situation where both parties win. Each party uses its energies and creativity to solve the problem at hand, not to beat the other party. This process involves identifying the problem at hand, the root cause of the problems at hand, analyzing several alternatives to solving the problem and finally choosing the best alternative.

2.3.6.4 Helping Conflicting Parties

To be helpful in conflicting parties, ensure that:

- You listen to the stories of both conflicting parties.
- Help each party to single out specific problems.
- Facilitate the parties to identify the root cause of their problem.
- Facilitate the parties to generate broad ideas on what could be done to solve the problem, taking into consideration the available opportunities.

2.3.7. Negotiation

Genesis 18:26-33 (NKJV), - So the LORD said, "If I find in Sodom fifty righteous within the city, then I will spare all the place for their sakes." Then Abraham answered and said, "Indeed now, I who am but dust and ashes have taken it upon myself to speak to the Lord: Suppose there were five less than the fifty righteous; would You destroy all of the city for lack of five?" So, He said, "If I find there forty-five, I will not destroy it." And he spoke to Him yet again and said, "Suppose there should be forty found there?" So, He said, "I will not do it for the sake of forty." Then he said, "Let not the Lord be angry, and I will speak: Suppose thirty should be found there?" So, He said, "I will not do it if I find thirty there." And he said, "Indeed now, I have taken it upon myself to speak to the Lord: Suppose twenty should be found there?" So, He said, "I will not destroy it for the sake of twenty." Then he said, "Let not the Lord be angry, and I will speak but once more: Suppose ten should be found there?" And He said, "I will not destroy it for the sake of ten." So, the LORD went His way as soon as He had finished speaking with Abraham; and Abraham returned to his place.

A common way that parties deal with conflict is via negotiation.

Define the term Negotiation

Negotiation can be defined in many ways including: -

- Negotiation is a discussion aimed at reaching an agreement on an issue, or
- Negotiation is a process whereby two or more parties work toward an agreement on an issue or matter.
- Negotiation is a dialogue between two or more people or parties to reach the desired outcome regarding one or more issues of conflict.

2.3.7.1 Stages of Negotiations

There are five stages of negotiation, namely investigation, determining your "best alternative to a negotiated agreement (BATNA), presentation, bargaining and closure.

(i) **Investigation** - this is information gathering stage, beginning with yourself: asking yourself for the goals for the negotiation? What you want to achieve? What would you concede? What would you absolutely not concede? Be brutally honest about your priorities. you'll inevitably be faced with making choices. Life is about taking and giving.

(ii) **Determine** - Your "best alternative to a negotiated agreement (BATNA) - This is an important stage to help you decide whether to accept an offer you receive during the negotiation. You need to know what your alternatives are. If you have various alternatives, you can look at the proposed deal more critically. Could you get a better outcome than the proposed deal? Your BATNA will help you reject an unfavorable deal. On the other hand, if the deal is better than another outcome you could get (that is, better than your BATNA), then you should accept it.

(iii) Presentation stage – In this stage. you assemble the information you've gathered in a way that supports the position or best alternative you have in the agreement.

(iv) Bargaining stage. In this stage, each party discusses their goals and seeks to get an agreement. A natural part of this process is making concessions, namely, giving up one thing to get something else in return. Making a concession is not a sign of weakness—parties expect to give up some of their goals. Rather, concessions demonstrate cooperativeness and help move the negotiation toward its conclusion. Making concessions is particularly important in tense disputes, which can get bogged down by old issues.

(v) Closure stage – at this stage, the negotiating parties have either come to an agreement on the terms, or one party has decided that the final offer is unacceptable and therefore must be walked away from. If your best offer has been rejected, it should serve as an opportunity to learn from, ask yourself what would have been taken to reach an amicable agreement.

2.3.7.2 Negotiating for implementation of community project.

- Always negotiate for qualified technical expertise for a fair price
- When buying property, you negotiate for the best value for your money.

2.3.8. Lobbying

Matthew 20:20-21 (NKJV) Then the mother of Zebedee's sons came to him with her sons, kneeling down and asking something from him. And he said to her, "what do you wish?" she said to him, "grant that these two sons of mine may sit, one on your right hand and the other on the left, in your kingdom."
The mother of Zebedee's son lobbying to ensure her sons have a position in Jesus's Kingdom.

Definition of the term lobbying

This is—

- Any attempt to influence a person in authority to give you a personal favour.
- Asking for help from a person in authority for a favour on behave of somebody else.

Benefits of lobbying

- You can request people in authority to help to solve personal problems – school fees, medical bills.
- You can lobby people in authority e.g., members of parliament or members of county assemblies to improve community social services e.g., improvement of road networks for marketing of community agricultural produce or Upgrade local health facilities for improved community health care or Increase opportunities for bursaries especially orphans and children from very humble backgrounds.

2.3.9. Advocacy

Mark 10.13 (NKJV). Then they brought little children to Him that he might touch them; but the disciples rebuked those who brought them. But when Jesus saw it, He was greatly displeased and said to them, "Let the little children come to Me and do not forbid them; for is the kingdom of God. I say to you, whoever does not receive the kingdom of God as a little child by no means enter it. And He took them up in His arms, laid His hands on them and blessed them. Jesus advocating for little children when denied access to Jesus.

Advocacy can be defined as follows

- Arguing in favour of somebody or an idea
- Public support given to somebody or a group of people for a good course or an idea that will benefit a community or group of people.
- Support, advice and help given to people who are unable to speak for themselves.

Examples of advocacy

- Advocacy program to help abused children or women.
- Advocacy program for children's rights
- Advocacy work aimed at creating opportunities for farmers e.g., fertilizer at affordable prices, access to the market.

Community advocacy helps people to feel enabled to take control of their own lives and provide practical support to overcome their social and economic issues.

2.3.10. Team Building in Groups

Nehemiah 4:15-23 (NKJV), And it happened, when our enemies heard that it was known to us, and that God had brought their plot to nothing, that all of us returned to the wall, everyone to his work. So it was, from that time on, that half of my servants worked at construction, while the other half held the spears, the shields, the bows, and wore armor; and the leaders were behind all the house of Judah. Those who built on the wall, and those who carried burdens, loaded themselves so that with one hand they worked at construction, and with the other held a weapon. Every one of the builders had his sword girded at his side as he built. And the one who sounded the trumpet was beside me. Then I said to the nobles, the rulers, and the rest of the people, "The work is great and extensive, and we are separated far from one another on the wall. Wherever you hear the sound of the trumpet, rally to us there. Our God will fight for us." So, we labored in the work, and half of the men held the spears from daybreak until the stars appeared. At the same time, I also said to the people, "Let each man and his servant stay at night in Jerusalem, that they may be our guard by night and a working party by day." So, neither I, my brethren, my servants, nor the men of the guard who followed me took off our clothes, except that everyone took them off for washing.

Nehemiah through teamwork rebuild the Wall of Jerusalem in the midst of their adversaries.

Definition of the term Team

A team is a group of people from diverse backgrounds having different skills and abilities, who work together with common purpose, goal and objectives.

Objective of Team Building

The main objective of team building is to create a feeling of interdependence and a sense of shared responsibility among the group to enable achievement of results. A good team;

- Communicates
- Co-operates
- Commits
- Contributes

Members' Roles in Team Building

Members role in team building is to; -

- Initiate the process of achieving a task-e.g., give ideas.
- Seek information required for effective reference.
- Provide needed information.
- Civil opinions
- Elaborate to clarify expected results.
- Harmonize, coordinate team ideas or activities.
- Summarize to highlight key conclusions on task performance.
- Being mindful of time as time is money.

2.3.11 Communication in Community Groups

Colossians 4:6 (NKJV), Let your speech always be with grace, seasoned with salt, that you may know how you ought to answer each one.

Ephesians 4:29 (NKJV), Let no corrupt word proceed out of your mouth, but what is good for necessary edification, that it may impart grace to the hearers.

Objectives of Communication

Communication is important in community groups because it facilitates collective action to achieve the groups' defined goals. Communication is defined as the process of transmitting information from one person to another person.

Effective communication is defined as the process of transmitting information and sharing the meaning of the message to achieve mutual understanding between the parties involved in the communication act.

Compare the communication in building the wall of Jerusalem (Nehemiah 4 God approved and supported until the wall was built and completed) and Building of the tower of Babel (Genesis 11.1-9. God disapproved confused the language of the builders and scattered them. Their mission was not achieved because of lack of effective communication).

Elements of Communication Process

Communication process consist of the following elements:

(i) **Sender/source** – a person who transmits message to another person or a group of people.

(ii) **Message** – is what is transmitted through a channel. The message should be brief, simple and clear in order to be understood and interpreted by the receiver. The message can be sent in any of the following forms:

- verbal – spoken.
- written – letter or report.
- visual (non-verbal)-gestures, pictures, diagrams, films, body language

(iii) **Channel** – it is what is used to transmit the message from sender/source to the receiver e.g.

- media for verbal messages
- telephone
- loudspeaker
- radio
- Television
- films/video

Non-Verbal Channels

- Dance
- Music
- Body language
- Facial expression

Symbolic Channels

- Artefacts
- Rituals
- Symbols of power or wealth
- Gifts

Print –Media

- Letters, memos
- Bulletins books, pamphlets
- Magazines, newspaper
- Minutes of meetings

(iv) Receiver – a person or persons who get information or message from the sender and continuously give feedback to the sender to confirm that the message has been received.

(v) Feedback – the return of information to the sender as a response to the message.

(vi) Encoding – converting the message the sender has into a form which can be understood by the receiver e.g., language used body movement written symbols etc.

(vii) Encoding – converting the message the sender has as a response to the message.

(viii) Decoding – involves interpretation of the message that has been received by the receiver to understand or have meaning.

Elements of Communication Diagrams

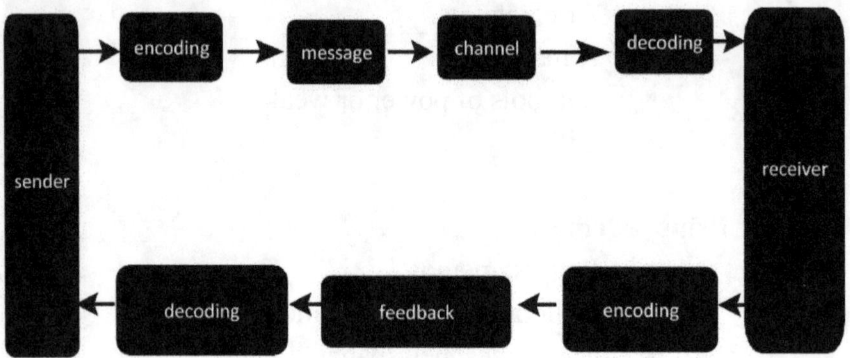

Noise (distortion)-is any kind of interference or factors which distort interpersonal and organizational communication.

(i) Exercise on Communication Process

Pair up with somebody

- Let each person take a paper and pen
- Each person holds the pen and without talking or gesturing draws a picture of a house.
- Allocate 5 minutes.
- Display the drawn pictures.
- what problems they experience as a pair drawing the house.
- What caused the problems?
- What led to the problem and why?
- Why did the communication breakdown?

Lessons learnt

- The communication was impossible without talking. We can never transfer 100% of what is in our minds into someone else's mind. The words we use do not exactly translate to thoughts. What you hear is not what was said or what was meant.
- We communicate all the time. We never stop sending messages to other people and receiving signals from them. In many cases we are not aware of the facts and consequently we do not control the process. We communicate silently.

(ii) Different Perceptions

(a)make nine dots and join them with four straight lines without lifting up their pens and without repeating any line.

(b) Demonstrate by use of five lines.

Plot five dots and try to join them

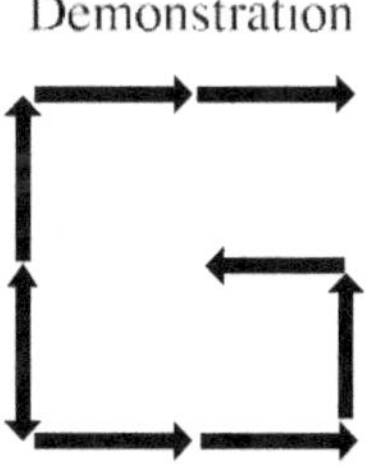

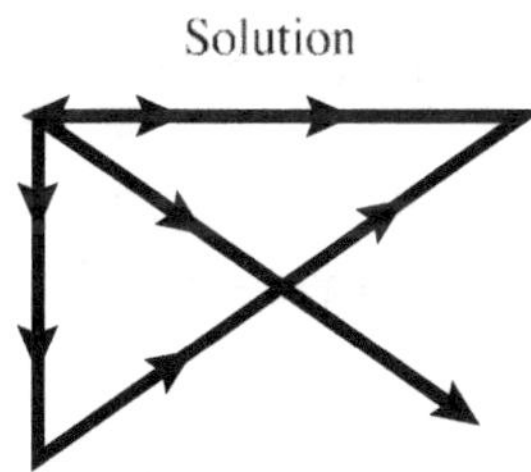

(c) Discuss why the exercise was impossible.

(d) Why did you see a square where there was no square

Lessons Learnt

(i) We limit our imagination, the information we receive has to fit into our norms, values and limited judgement.

(ii) We see things that are not there, we build walls around us.

(iii) Our perceptions are different. It is not easy to explain to others what is obvious to us.

(iv) Information distorts the meaning, we select, we screen, we add and subtract, as it suits us.

Purpose of Communication

The purpose of communication in community groups is to make people act, change, and achieve desired goals.

Act – translate words into action. This shows the message was understood.

Change – make someone understand better ways of doing things.

Achieve – change or influence peoples' thinking and doing of things differently to achieve what they want.

Barriers to Communication

There are many barriers which take place. These barriers include:

(i) Age Difference

Age differences between the sender and the receiver e.g., young field officers often fail to communicate effectively with village elders, making it difficult to get development messages across.

(ii) Economic Gap

Between diverse groups e.g., field officers advising farmers in poor locality to use tractors when they cannot even afford to use ploughs.

(iii) Language

Use of technical language to a group of laymen who have no previous experience in the subject.

(iv) Attitudes of Senders or Receivers

If the attitude is positive, effective communication will take place: if attitude is negative, no effective communication.

(v) **Social/Cultural Differences**.

Different social/cultural practices and believes can hinder effective communication e.g., woman should not address a gathering. This poses a problem for female officers.

(vi) Competition for Attention

To be an effective communicator, you must be able to catch the audiences' attention and hold it throughout the period of presentation. Lack of co-ordination often restricted in creating conflicts of interest and attention to various development activities e.g., development workers visiting villages simultaneously without coordination.

Villagers are expected to attend the various development programs, for example health campaigns or introducing new agricultural practices.

How to Overcome Barriers to Communication

Barriers to communication can be overcome in the following ways:

(i) The sender must know the audiences' backgrounds, interests, language and needs. The people with whom the sender communicates with should act, think, understand and adapt the things he/she wants them to do.

(a) Every member is unique. Each person responds to sender's message according to his own drive, attitudes and motivation, their educational and social background and interests. One must understand human nature and needs. Use the languages that the audience understands.

(ii) The message must be timely, meaningful and applicable to the situation.

(a) It is meaningless to talk about the advantages of using audio-visual aids without using any such examples during presentation.

(b) It's untimely for a health worker to try to convince a group to do something about one disease when an outbreak of another is taking place in an adjacent area.

(c) Deliver messages at the right time and place e.g., it is easier to persuade people to dig pit latrines during cholera epidemic.

(iii) The audience /receiver must overcome their personal barriers. Typical personalities creating barriers to communication include:

(a) The non-listeners –refuse to listen or if they do, they do not do it inattentively.

(b) The know-it all: the characters think they know everything and have ready answers to every question.

(c) The negative personality –says no to everything except their ideas.

(d) The impatient person cannot sit throughout a presentation. They jump to conclusions.

2.3.12 Leadership in Community Groups

Exodus 18:17-23 (NKJV) So Moses' father-in-law said to him, "The thing that you do is not good. Both you and these people who are with you will surely wear yourselves out. For this thing is too much for you; you are not able to perform it by yourself. Listen now to my voice; I will give you counsel, and God will be with you: Stand before God for the people, so that you may bring the difficulties to God. And you shall teach them the statutes and the laws, and show them the way in which they must walk and the work they must do. Moreover, you shall select from all the people able men, such as fear God, men of truth, hating covetousness; and place such over them to be rulers of thousands, rulers of hundreds, rulers of fifties, and rulers of tens. And let them judge the people at all times. Then it will be that every great matter they shall bring to you, but every small matter they themselves shall judge. So it will be easier for you, for they will bear the burden with you. If you do this thing, and God so commands you, then you will be able to endure, and all this people will also go to their place in peace."
As a leader, are you doing everything by yourself or delegating to other people?

Definition of the term leadership

(i) Leadership is defined as the art of mobilizing, organizing and guiding a community group in order to achieve their defined goals.

(ii) It is also the ability to effectively guide and influence the community to reach their defined goals.

Qualities of Leadership

Qualities of good leadership include:

- Intelligence
- Strong character and courage
- Creativeness and innovativeness
- Good decision making
- Getting things done though other people
- Simplicity and flexibility

Leadership Styles

Leadership style is the different ways leaders govern people. The main leadership styles include:

- Dictatorship/authoritative leadership
- Lazier –faire (free-rein) leadership
- Democratized leadership

(i) Dictatorship/authoritative leadership

Characteristics of this style of leadership include: -

- Orders flow from the top, and people must obey without question.
- People have no role in decision-making.
- Decisions from above are implemented without input.
- The leader decides what is best for everyone.
- The leader has full control and makes all decisions.
- People's feelings or self-image are ignored.

Advantages

Dictatorship/authoritative leadership is useful in emergency situations where decisions have to be made quickly and swift action taken to save the situation.

Disadvantages

(i) It removes people's confidence and promotes suspicion, division and mistrust.
(ii) It does not encourage participation and creative thinking.
(iii) People may abandon the group if their views are not considered.

(ii) Lazier-Faire (free-rein) Leadership

Characteristics of this leadership style include:

- People are left free to do whatever they want at their own time and convenience.
- The leader has no control and is only a leader by name.
- Leadership is inefficient and irresponsible and decisions are made by chance.
- Chances for group success are remote.

Advantages

(i) It is best in a situation of possible conflict mitigation where the leader does not want to take sides but rather remain non-committal because of possible consequences.
(ii) Can be used to save a leader from danger or embarrassment in a situation of dilemma.

Disadvantages

(i) It lowers people's morale.
(ii) It promotes disunity within the group.
(iii) Makes leadership to look like it has no authority, direction or decisiveness.

(iii) Democratic Leadership

Democratic leadership is characterized by: -

- Leaders promoting participatory decision making.
- Each person is regarded as equal and the opinions of every person are respected as well as considered in the process of decision making.
- Decisions made are binding, lasting and uniting.
- It empowers the leader and the community.

Advantages

(i) Responsibilities and initiatives are promoted as people's views are taken seriously.

(ii) Democracy gives people the opportunity to make a real contribution to the development process.

(iii) Provides people with the right to distribute and use power.

Disadvantages

(i) Decision making can be a slow process.

(ii) Freedom may be abused.

(iii) Freedom may easily be mistaken for weak leadership.

MODULE 3

COMMUNITY SITUATION ANALYSIS

3.1 Introduction

Community Situation Analysis is a process that critically looks at the community needs and resources in order to set a plan for sustainable development.

Community situation analysis helps the community to answer the question "Where are we now" it gives a vivid picture of their current situation.

2 Kings 7:3-10 (NIV) Now there were four men with leprosy at the entrance of the city gate. They said to each other, "Why stay here until we die? If we say, 'We'll go into the city'—the famine is there, and we will die. And if we stay here, we will die. So let's go over to the camp of the Arameans and surrender. If they spare us, we live; if they kill us, then we die." At dusk they got up and went to the camp of the Arameans. When they reached the edge of the camp, no one was there, for the Lord had caused the Arameans to hear the sound of chariots and horses and a great army, so that they said to one another, "Look, the king of Israel has hired the Hittite and Egyptian kings to attack us!" So they got up and fled in the dusk and abandoned their tents and their horses and donkeys. They left the camp as it was and ran for their lives. The men who had leprosy reached the edge of the camp, entered one of the tents and ate and drank. Then they took silver, gold and clothes, and went off and hid them. They returned and entered another tent and took some things from it and hid them also.

The lepers analyzing their situation and deciding on the course of action to save themselves in a sustainable way.

3.2 Objectives

By the end of this module, the participants would have acquired skills on:

- Identification and prioritization of community needs/problems.
- Problem tree analysis
- S.W.O.T. analysis
- Stakeholder analysis
- Gender issues
- Governance issues

3.3. Identification and Prioritization of Community Needs /Problems

(i) Identify your community needs/problems and list them down.

(ii) Prioritize the need/problems i.e., list the problems according to the order of the most pressing need and in which they wish to solve fast, then the second problem, third problem etc. up to the last problem

(iii) Identify obstacles that would prevent solving prioritized problems.

(iv) Identify all the resources available in the community

(v) Facilitate participants to show them how they can use the available resources to solve their problems.

3.4. Problem Tree Analysis

Problem tree analysis is a method used to analyze the root causes of problems in a community and effects of those problems on the community.

(i) What is your first priority of problems that should be addressed first in your community e.g., poverty. Poverty becomes the focal problem i.e., one that relates/ creates other problems.

(ii) Think critically about how a problem (e.g., poverty) impacts/affects the community.

(iii) Examine the cause of the problem (e.g., poverty) –this will be the roots of the problem (root cause)

(iv) Examine the effects of the problem on the people – the branches. E.g., The root/main problem in the community –poverty

The branches/Effects of the problem – lack of food, lack of school fees, lack of good clothes

Problem Tree Diagram

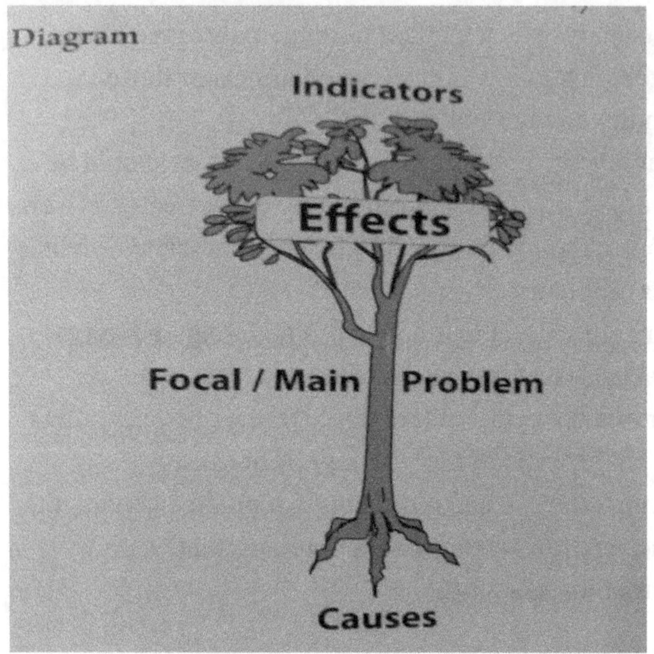

For example – Poverty as Focal/main problem

(i) Cause of poverty – root cause

Possibly the main causes of poverty

- Unfavorable weather conditions
- Insecurity
- Illiteracy
- Lack of money
- Ill health.

(ii) Effects of Poverty - branches

Possible effect of poverty on the community

- Food Insecurity
- Robbery, Thugs
- Low School Enrollment
- Teenage pregnancies mothers
- Early marriages
- High School Dropouts
- High Death Rates
- Lack of Basic Needs.

(iii) Activities

These are proposed solutions to causes of the main problem (poverty) e.g.

- Irrigation
- Projects Community
- Security Arrangements
- Adult Education Classes Education
- Bursary Funds
- Income Generating Activities
- Preventive Health.

(iv)Outputs

These are the indicators of achievements, showing the impact/benefits of the solutions of the problems to the community, e.g.

- Food Security
- Safe and Secure Environment
- High School Enrollment
- Low School's Dropouts
- Low Death Rates
- Provision of Basic Needs

3.5 S.W.O.T Analysis

Judges 6.11-15 (NKJV) - Now the Angel of the Lord came and sat under the terebinth tree which was in Ophrah, which belonged to Joash the Abiezrite, while his son Gideon threshed wheat in the winepress, in order to hide it from the Midianites. And the Angel of the Lord appeared to him, and said to him, "The Lord is with you, you mighty man of valor!" Gideon said to Him, "O my lord, if the Lord is with us, why then has all this happened to us? And where are all His miracles which our fathers told us about, saying, 'Did not the Lord bring us up from Egypt?' But now the Lord has forsaken us and delivered us into the hands of the Midianites." Then the Lord turned to him and said, "Go in this might of yours, and you shall save Israel from the hand of the Midianites. Have I not sent you?" So he said to Him, "O my Lord, how can I save Israel? Indeed, my clan is the weakest in Manasseh, and I am the least in my father's house."

What lessons do you learn from this scripture?

Case study

Youth at Mwamba village are focused, hardworking, enterprising and ambitious. Surprisingly, only one of them is a university graduate, two are diploma holders, ten are certificate holders and the rest are semi-illiterate. They recently visited a regional agriculture show and discovered to their amazement that they can expand their horticulture project to grow a variety of vegetables for export market. They learned at the show that vegetables grown organically have a high demand in the export market.

However, their constraints were the technical know-how of growing vegetables organically, the operations of export market and lack funds for transporting the vegetables into the export market. Fortunately, in the neighboring district, there is an SME organization willing to guide them on the basics of organic farming, how to grow vegetables for export market and also give them loan to start the business. The SME operations are in line with the government policy of economic empowerment of the youth and promotion of small business in the rural areas.

In spite of this, the youth are still a worried lot. What is on their minds is how to overcome the cutthroat competition in the export market. What if the water in their borehole diminishes considering the unpredictability of the rainfall? Will group members stick together in times of difficulties? Nevertheless, the youth were ready to give the project a try as their motto is the sky is the limit.

Discussions

(i) What are the youth's individual good points?
(ii) What are their individual limitations?
(iii) Is there a chance for them to be helped address these limitations?
(iv) What are the key reasons that would make their project not succeed?

What do you understand the term S.W.O.T and explain the importance of S.W.O.T. analysis.

SWOT stands for

S - Strengths –within the community/self (internal)
W - Weakness –when the community /self (internal)
O. - Opportunities –outside the community/(external)
T - Threats –outside the community / (external)

The purpose of S.W.O.T. analysis is to help community members /individuals to see their current strengths, weaknesses, opportunities and threats of their community in regard to sustainable development.

Strengths

Are positive aspects that exist within the community (internal issues). The aim is to identify them and build on them to achieve community objectives and goals. Strengths reflect community resources and community members' contributions. E.g.

- Hard working and cooperative individuals
- Educated and skilled people in the community
- Availability of community resources-sand stones water trees
- Individual wealth
- Healthy people.

Weaknesses

Are the negative aspects within the community (internal issues) Community members should seek to overcome the weaknesses e.g.

- Inequalities within the community
- Gender imbalances
- Negative attitudes, values, retrogressive customs of community members.
- Illiteracy
- Unwillingness to work hard.

Opportunities

Are chances that occur in the external environment that the community can access and use to bring out sustainable development their community The community should strive to see available opportunities and see how to use them to help the community achieve its objectives and goals e.g.

- Donors and NGOs Support
- Cross Border Trade
- Government Willingness to Support Community Initiatives
- Existing government development programs.

Threats

Are obstacles in the external environment that may hinder or interfere with community efforts to bring about sustainable development. The community must be aware of them and strategize on how to manage them e.g.

- unforeseen failure-change in government
- risk in community –insecurity, high level corruption
- lack of donor support
- Frequent incidents of natural calamities; floods drought.

Exercise

1. Identify a pressing problem in a community e.g., Provision of clean water.
2. Draw four quadrants.
3. Label them strengths, weaknesses, opportunities, and threats.

Filling the quadrants using the following guiding questions in regard to provision of clean water in the community: -

(a) What are the community's major strengths?
(b) What are their major weaknesses?
(c) What are their major opportunities?
(d) What are their major threats?

S.W.O.T. analysis in provision of clean water

Strengths e.g. Retired water experts Natural streams	**Opportunity e.g.** Available government funds Presence of NGOs
Weaknesses e.g., Disunity Unwillingness to do manual work	**Threats e.g.,** Insecurity Unpredictable conditions.

3.6 Stakeholder Analysis

Stakeholders are individuals, groups or institutions that have interest in a project and can influence its success or failure, e.g., in provision of clean water. stakeholders can be categorized as:

(i) Primary stakeholders

Are those stakeholders directly affected either positively or negatively by the project the e.g., in a water project these are men, women, children, herders.

(ii) Secondary stakeholders

Are the intermediaries in the project process, including both winners and losers, involved and excluded groups, e.g., indirect project beneficiaries and those excluded from the project benefits.

(iii) Key stakeholders

Are those who significantly influence or are important to the success of the project, e.g., community members, government ministries of water, environment, health, survey, municipalities, NGOs with projects in community development, environment, and health.

3.6.1 Reasons for Stakeholder Analysis

To identify all the people, groups, institutions who

(i) Have interest in the project and can contribute to its implementation e.g., provide materials, funds and professional advice.

(ii) Can directly contribute to the project implementation, administration and management.

(iii) Can participate in monitoring and evaluating project activities.

Exercise

(a) Identify stakeholders in your area for provision of clean water project in the following categories:

- Community
- Government Agencies
- NGOs
- Donors

(b) What are the identified stakeholders' current activities?

(c) How can they contribute or participate in the provision of clean water project in your area?

3.7 Governance Issues

Genesis 47:13-26 (NKJV) - Now there was no bread in all the land; for the famine was very severe, so that the land of Egypt and the land of Canaan languished because of the famine. And Joseph gathered up all the money that was found in the land of Egypt and in the land of Canaan, for the grain which they bought;; and Joseph brought the money into Pharaoh's house So when the money failed in the land of Egypt and in the land of Canaan, all the Egyptians came to Joseph and said, "Give us bread, for why should we die in your presence? For the money has failed. "Then Joseph said, "Give your livestock, and I will give you bread for your livestock, if the money is gone. "So they brought their livestock to Joseph, and Joseph gave them bread and exchange for the horses, the flocks, the cattle of the herds, and for the donkeys. Thus he fed them with bread in exchange for all their livestock that year. When that year had ended, they came to him the next year and said to him, "We will not hide from my lord that our money is gone; my lord also has our herds of livestock. There is nothing left in the sight of my lord but our bodies and our lands. Why should we die before your eyes, both we and our land? Buy us and our land for bread, and we and our land will be servants of Pharaoh; give us seed, that we may live and not die, that the land may not be desolate." Then Joseph bought all the land of Egypt for Pharaoh; for every man of the Egyptians sold his field, because the famine was severe upon them. So the land became Pharaoh's. And as for the people, he moved them into the cities, from one end of the borders of Egypt to the other end. Only the land of the priests he did not buy; for the priests had rations allotted to them by Pharaoh, and they ate their rations which Pharaoh gave them; therefore, they did not sell their lands Then Joseph said

to the people, "Indeed I have bought you and your land this day for Pharaoh. Look here is seed for you, and you shall sow the land. And it shall come to pass in the harvest that you shall give one-fifth to Pharaoh. Four-fifths shall be your own, as seed for the field and for your food, for those of your households and as food for your little ones." So they said, "You have saved our lives;; let us find favor in the sight of my lord, and we will be Pharaoh's servants." And Joseph made it a law over the land of Egypt to this day, that Pharaoh should have one-fifth, except for the land of the priests only, which did not become Pharaoh's.

3.7.1. Definition of the term Governance

Governance is defined as the exercise of economic, political, and administrative authority in the management of a country's affairs at all levels i.e., at individual, family, community and national levels.

3.7.2 Importance of Learning About Governance

- To identify governance issues that could affect the design and implementation of community projects for sustainable development.
- To understand that every citizen has a basic right to play a full role in the society, participate fully in societal affairs and make decisions on matters pertaining to their material and social affairs.
- Individual citizens have the right to play their full social roles to achieve a basic state of well-being, irrespective of their race, color, sex, ethnic group, language age, religion, political affiliation, disability or any other circumstances.

3.7.3 Key Governance Dimensions (Aspects)

Different governance dimensions /aspects include

(i) Political Governance

This involves decision making and policy implementation by legitimate authority which represents the interests of the society and allows citizens to freely make decisions such as electing their representatives at all levels.

(ii) Economic Governance

This involves the process of decision making with respect to economic activities e.g. Business startups and ownership. Means of livelihood e.g., agriculture, livestock keeping. Influence on society's issues such as equity, poverty, and quality of life.

(iii) Administrative Governance

It involves an administrative system i.e.,
Efficient – careful use of resources.
Accountable – accounting for use of resources.
Impartial – treating everybody equally without taking sides.

(iv) Systematic Governance

This includes the structure and systems of the society 'which guide political and socio-economic relationships, protect cultural and religious values and creates an enabling environment for sustainable improvement of quality life.

3.7.4 Qualities of Good Governance Good governance should be:

(i) Participatory

So that all stakeholders take an active part in decision making and contribute to their activities as citizens.

(ii) Transparent

So that all stakeholders have access to information about the community or government decisions e.g., projects to implemented in the community i.e., where the water project will be implemented, who will fund, how much money approved for the project, who will manage the project.

(iii). Accountable

So that all stakeholders including the community, NGOs, government are accountable to the community for their designs and actions e.g., project activities implemented and the amount of money spent.

(iv) Effective

So that government and community resources are used wisely to address community needs/problems and priorities in order to achieve set objectives and goals.

(v) Equitable

So that all sectors of the society have equal access to benefits of services and decision-making processes without any discrimination upon their gender, social status, ethnic grouping, age etc.

Example: Governance issues in water project

Identify issues in the provision of clean water projects in your area and how they affect project implementation and suggest intervention strategies as tabulated below e.g.

Governance issues	How they affect project implementation	Intervention strategy
1. Lack of community participation in project identification and implementation	Lack of ownership Vandalism Sabotage Abandonment Failure of operation and maintenance	Community consultation Enhance community ownership. Community participation in leadership, management
2. Political interferences	Political support for project implementation	Consultation with community and their political leaders
3. Poor support from government	Lack of continuity and stalling of projects. Disinterest from the community and mist	Build partnership with community and government. Build confidence and trust with community.

3.8 Corruption

Proverbs 15.27 (NKJV). He who is greedy for gain troubles his own house. But he who hate bribes will live

Exodus 23.8(NKJV) and you shall not take no bribe for a bribe blinds the discerning and prevents the words of the discerning

3.8.1. Definition of corruption

Corruption can be defined in many ways as follows:

- Corruption is the abuse of entrusted power for private benefits and gains.
- Dishonest or illegal behavior especially by powerful people (such as government officials, NGO officials, community leaders or church leaders
- Inducement to wrong by improper or unlawful means (such as bribery) the corruption of government official
- Corruption is dishonest conduct by those in positions of power in both public and private sectors for personal benefit and gains.
- Corruption is a form of dishonesty or a criminal offense which is undertaken by a person or an organization which is entrusted in a position of authority, in order to acquire illicit benefits or abuse power for one's personal gain.
- A departure from the original or from what is pure or correct.

3.8.2. Forms of Corruption

Corruption involves giving or accepting a bribe, favors, inappropriate gifts, double-dealing, under-the-table transactions;

- Election manipulation;
- Diversion of public funds;
- Money laundering;
- Defrauding of investors;
- Giving kickbacks;
- Doubling contractual project's amounts;
- Doing sub-standards works on public projects are all forms of corruption.

3.8.3 Impact of Corruption

- Corruption erodes trust.
- Weakens democracy.
- Hampers economic development.
- Further exacerbates inequality, poverty, social division and the environmental crisis.

Exercise

Describe incidences of corruption in your area and impact on sustainable community development.

3.9 Gender Analysis

Genesis 1:26-27 (NKJV) Then God said, "Let Us make man in Our image, according to Our likeness; let them have dominion over the fish of the sea, over the birds of the air, and over the cattle, over all the earth and over every creeping thing that creeps on the earth." So God created man in His own image; in the image of God He created him; male and female He created them.

Genesis 2:18 (NKJV). And the LORD God said, "It is not good that man should be alone; I will make him a helper comparable to him."

Case study

Haika comes from a very humble background. Her family, father, mother, two brothers and three sisters barely struggle through life by engaging in subsistence farming on their two- acre farm. Luckily through the government subsidized secondary education, all her siblings including herself are in school.

Haika always looks forward to school holidays because that is the chance to visit her aunty who lives in the neighboring district. Her aunt's husband operates a successful business at the nearby shopping center and they also keep dairy cattle and grow fruits and vegetables on their farm for home consumption and sale of the surplus.

Her aunt's family consists of six members: herself, her husband, her two daughters and her two sons. Haika has a lot of admiration for their way of life. All family members work on strict schedules of work. Their day starts at 5:30 am. Her uncle starts the day by supervising the workers as they milk the cows and weigh the milk for delivery at the local dairy.

After that he moves to the horticultural garden to allocate duties for the day to the workers, including his children. Meanwhile her aunt would be busy in the kitchen with one of their sons or daughters preparing breakfast. After breakfast her uncle leaves to attend to his shop, while the rest of the family goes back to the farm. At lunch break her aunt and her cousins prepare lunch and serve everybody. As the cousins wash utensils and attend to other family chores, her aunt takes food to her uncle and also assists him in attending to customers till evening when they come home together.

Back in her village the story is completely different. The women wake up early to sweep the compounds. They then go to fetch water in the nearby river to make breakfast and serve to the men sitting outside the main house. Culturally, it is a taboo for men to go in or near the kitchen or having anything to do with preparing and serving food. After breakfast, the men go to nearby shopping center for a chat with friends or visit relatives in the nearby villages.

The women go to cultivate the farms till evening. On their way home they pluck vegetables and collect firewood for preparing the evening meal. Women are wholly responsible for domestic chores and cultivating the fields including marketing of farm produce. interestingly after sale of farm produce the women hand over all the money to their husbands or elder sons who in turn decide how much they give back to the women for housekeeping.

Discussion

1. What are the defined roles and responsibilities of women and men in your community?
2. How does this division of labor between men and women impact on the development of the community?

3.9.1. Definition of Gender concepts.

(i) Gender
(ii) Sex
(iii) Gender awareness/sensitive
(iv) Gender planning
(v) Gender balance
(vi) Gender equity

(i) Gender

Refers to characteristics of men and women that socially/culturally determined, unlike or in contrast to those which are biologically determined (sex). It refers to roles and responsibilities and behavior of men and women in the day –to-day social, cultural, economic and political contexts.

(ii) Sex

Sex is a biological term used to determine whether one is female or male. You are born male or female and sometimes on rare occasion both female and male organs.

(iii) Gender awareness/sensitivity

Gender awareness/sensitivity is having knowledge about issues /challenges that affect men and women in a community.

(iv) Gender planning: planning for development programs to include both men and women.

(v) Gender balance: Development programs that have a balance between men and women.

(vi) Gender equity: Development programs that give equal opportunities or chances to both men and women.

3.9.2 Purpose of Gender Awareness and Analysis

Explain the importance of gender awareness and analysis.

(i) To increase awareness about gender issues/challenges by looking at how projects can affect the role of men and women in a community.

(ii) It is a means by which communities can improve their gender balance in planning and implementing development projects.

3.9.3. How Gender is Determined and taught

(i) Rules of behavior are given to girls and boys, men and women by their society, e.g.

(ii) How they are expected to dress, speak and act as well as the work they are expected to do and how they should interact /relate with each other.

(iii) Gender roles and behaviour are taught verbally from birth, for example, the birth of a boy child often leads to a celebration while the birth of a girl child may be greeted with indifferences and sadness.

(iv) Many parents treat male and female children differently e.g. Boys are encouraged to be active and aggressive Girls are encouraged to be passive and submissive.

Describe your own experiences of being born a boy or girl and how you were expected to behave.

3.9.4. Gender Roles and Responsibilities

Analyze gender roles and responsibilities using the exercise below and draw conclusions about your findings.

(i) Ask participants to list down all activities done by men and women from the time they wake up to the time they retire to bed at night.

(ii) Ask participants to list down roles and responsibilities on separate sheets of paper labeled women, men.

(iii) Swoop over the labels women to men and men to women e.g.

(i) Women –first list of roles	(i) Men-first list of roles
(ii) Men-swooped roles	(ii)Women- swooped roles

(iv) Discuss the roles and responsibilities that CANNOT physically be done by men and those that CANNOT physically be done by women after swooping labels. (women to men and men to women)

(v) Ask participants to discuss the roles or functions that are biologically determined and circle them. Discuss the factors that determine the different roles or functions for men and women that are not biologically determined.

(vi) Ask participants to conclude their findings.

The conclusion should include:

1. Women do all work, occupying their lives than men, especially during their day-to-day work.

2. Traditional roles and responsibilities can be done by both men and women except that some roles are better done either by men or women.

3. Only biological roles of bearing children can be done only by men or women. e.g.
   - Only men can provide seed to make children.
   - Only women can carry babies in their wombs for nine months and give birth to babies and breast feed them.

4. Men and women should share their roles and responsibilities equally except the ones that are biologically determined. Sharing roles equally between men and women promotes sustainable development.
5. Understanding gender differences helps in creating awareness to the way in which communities place men and women and categorize their roles and responsibilities.
6. It helps in learning ways in which gender roles and responsibilities can be the basis of both cooperation and conflict among men and women and development of appropriate strategies.

3.9.5 Gender Division of Labour

Definition of the concept of Gender Division of Labor.
Gender division of labor refers to the different kinds of work done by men and women and different values attached to the work. The work done by men and women is categorized as follows:

- Men's work –work done mostly by men e.g., outdoor activities.
- Women's work –work done mostly by women e.g.in-house activities.
- Productive labor – work that creates goods and services e.g., cultivating food crops and, marketing, herding cattle.
- Reproductive labor- work that is done mostly by women e.g.
  - childbearing and rearing
  - home keeping-fetching water, providing food cleaning.
  - providing physical and emotional needs of the family

Work performed predominantly by men is usually given higher status and also higher pay than that done pre-dominantly by women. Women's work is given lower status and lower pay.

Differences in evaluating men's work and women's' work shows inequality between men and women.

Importance of Studying Gender Division of Labor

It is important to study and understand gender division of labor because:

(i) It helps the community to understand the work done by both men and women in its social/cultural context and how development projects affect men and women. There should be equal opportunities for both men and women.

(ii) It demonstrates how women and men roles and responsibilities relate to each other. The roles should complement each other and not compete.

(iii) It clarifies the interdependence and cooperation among men and women. There should be strong partnership between men and women for faster progress and development.

(iv) It shows what inequalities and conflict exist among men and women. Inequalities and conflicts, if left unresolved slows down progress and development, mitigation strategies should be put in place to address them.

(v) It helps in understanding the relationship between men and women and proper planning for inclusive development. It also helps in identifying assistance needed by men and women in their development agenda.

Gender Access and Control

Numbers 27.4-8 (NKJV) – why should the name of our father be removed from among his family because he had no son? Give us a possession among our father's brother. So Moses brought their case before the Lord. And the Lord spoke to Moses saying, "The daughter of Zelophehad speak what is right;; you shall surely give them a possession of inheritance among their father's brothers and cause the inheritance of their father pass to them. And you shall speak to the children of Israel saying, "if a man dies and has no son, then you shall cause his inheritance to pass to his daughter"

Exercise

Describe how inheritance issues are handled in your community, as regards to widows, widowers, sons and daughters

Definition of gender access and control profile

Gender access and control profile is a tool used to show difference between women and men in terms of who has access to and control over the resources (land, money) necessary to perform their roles and responsibilities and also the benefits accruing from performing them.

Exercise

Analyze, access and control of community resources and who benefits from them and draw a conclusion. Tabulate results as below e.g.

Gender access and control profile

Resource	Access		Control		Benefit	
	Men	Women	Men	Women	Men	Women
Land	✓	✓	✓		✓	✓
Money	✓	✓	✓	✓	✓	✓
House	✓	✓	✓		✓	✓
Education	✓	✓	✓		✓	✓
Livestock	✓		✓		✓	

Conclusion from findings

1. Women may have access to some resources such as land and livestock but lack control over them. Women are not able to make the decisions on how resources should be used. their access to the benefits of these resources is also restricted.

2. Because women generally work longer hours than men, they have less access to time than me. This restricts women's access to social services and benefits such as schooling and training which could open up new life opportunities .in most cases, women are disadvantaged.

3. The access and control profile shows the power relationships within the community and what power is built on. Power centralized over resources such as land, livestock and children and also social status and political prestige. The one who controls most resources forms good partnership which is required for faster progress and development.

MODULE 4

COMMUNITY ACTION PLANNING

("where do we want to go")

4.1 Introduction

Deuteronomy 2:1-3 (NASB, 1995), where Moses says: "Then we turned and set out for the wilderness by the way to the Red Sea, as the LORD spoke to me, and circled Mount Seir for many days. "And the LORD spoke to me, saying, 'You have circled this mountain long enough. Now turn north,

Deuteronomy 1:6-8 (NKJV), "The LORD our God spoke to us in Horeb, saying: 'You have dwelt long enough at this mountain. Turn and take your journey, and go to the mountains of the Amorites, to all the neighboring places in the plain, in the mountains and in the lowland, in the South and on the seacoast, to the land of the Canaanites and to Lebanon, as far as the great river, the River Euphrates. See, I have set the land before you; go in and possess the land which the LORD swore to your father.

Have you or your community stayed in the current situation for a long time? Where do you or the community want to move to?

After the community analyzes their situation from different aspects and identifies the root cause of their problems, the next step is to plan for actions to get them out of their negative state affairs to a positive state. This begins with the community identifying a vision as people without vision perish. Community action planning answers the question, **"where do we want to go."** ***(Refer to Wata Constituency Case Study)***
Refer to the start of development in your area.

What can be done to improve the situation?

4.2 Objectives

At the end of this module, the participants will be able to

1. Explain the concept of vision building.
2. Describe how to set goals and achieve a vision.
3. Describe how to set objectives to achieve goals.
4. Identify activities to achieve set objectives.
5. Conceptualize the link between vision, goal, objectives and activities.
6. Develop a community action plan for development.

4.3. Definition of the term vision

Proverbs 29.18 (KJV)- Where there is no Vision, the people perish.

Why is it important to have vision? Give an example of a vision statement

Vision is looking beyond the current negative community problems (e.g., poverty, diseases, lack of food) to a positive outcome/result (e.g., wealthy and healthy people living in abundance) for a specified period of time, e.g., 5-10 years. It answers the question, "What do we want the community to be in 5-10 years' time to come"

Or in what state do you want the community to be in 5-10 years?

Vision Building

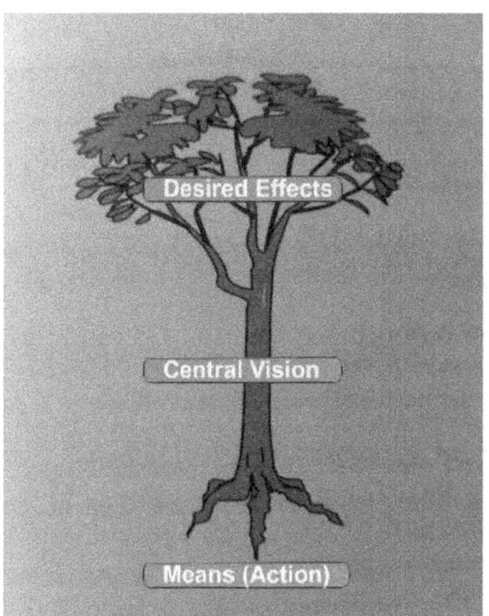

Examples of vision statements

(i) Improved standards of living in a community
(ii) Poverty reduction in a community

4.4. Goal setting – How do we get there?

Explain the term goal?

Why is it important to set goals? Give an example of a goal statement

- Goals are solutions to identified problems in order to achieve vision. Goals contribute to realization of a vision.
- A goal is a simple statement of where the community is trying to get to in a particular time e.g. Have a healthy community by 2025.
- Goals answer the question "How do we get to our vision."

4.5 Setting Objectives

Define the term Objective and explain why it is important to set objectives. Give an example of an objective.

The term objective can be defined in many different ways including,

- Objectives are stepping stones to goals, i.e., they help to achieve goals.
- Objectives are derived from problems that the project is designed to address.
- Objectives are what to do in order to achieve a goal.

General Principles of setting an objective is that they should be **SMART i.e**.

Specific – The statement must be of desired results specific.

Measurable – The desired result can be measured by indicators in numbers/quantity.

Attainable - -the community should be able to achieve the desired results as they implement the project, i.e., the expected results should not be too ambitious that it cannot be achieved.

Result Oriented – clearly specify the desired results. What you want to give

Time bound – Must have a time frame in which to complete the project, i.e. Have a target date by which the project should be achieved.

Examples of **SMART** Objectives

1. Reduce infant mortality by 10% by 2025, in Mayani County
2. Provide clean drinking water to 200 families by 2025 in Mayani County
3. Ensure food security to 200 families by 2025, in Mayani County

4.6. Identifying Activities

Explain the term activity as used in a project

Why is it important to identify activities for set objectives in a project?

The term activity as used in a project is the action taken to achieve the set objectives e.g.

Objective – To reduce infant mortality rate 10% by year 2025

Activities to be taken to achieve the above objective will be:

(i) Purchase medical equipment and drugs for the local health center.
(ii) Post qualified medical staff to local health centers
(iii) Initiate child immunization programs. Create awareness on the importance of child immunization.
(iv) Initiate demonstrations on child development milestones during immunization days.

4.7. Conceptualized links of vision, goals, objectives and activities

Draw a diagram showing links between vision, goals, objectives and activities.

Diagrams drawn should be as below:

Goal, Objectives, Activities Link

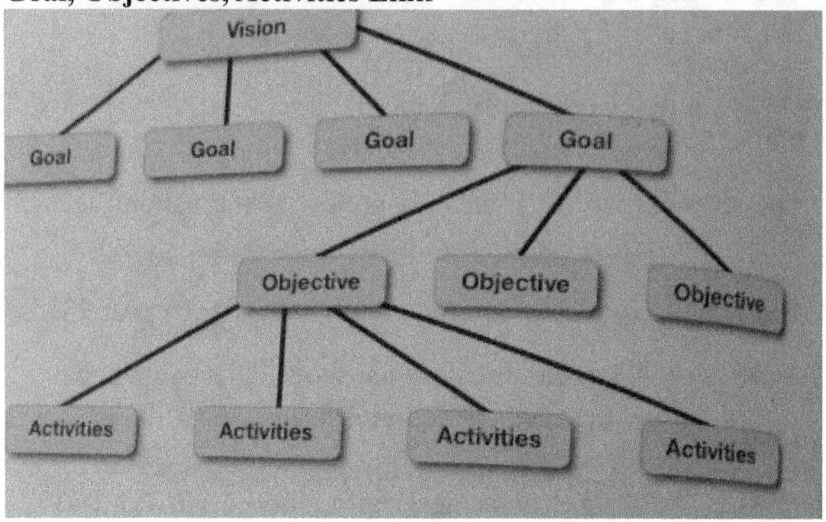

4.8 Community Action Plan for Development

Explain what you understand by the concept of Community Action Plan (CAP) and describe what is contained in the CAP. Draw a CAP for the community.

(i) A Community Action Plan (CAP) is a summary of all the community's development priorities which are used as a basis for planning for sustainable development.

(ii) Community Action Plan contains

- Vision – vision gives the overall direction for the CAP.
- Goals – goals help to achieve/realize the vision.
- Objectives – objectives help to achieve /realize goals Objective should be **(SMART)**
- Activities – these help to achieve/realize objectives.
- Consensus on who will do what, when and where.
- Identified resources required for the project and when.
- Estimated project budget and funds.
- Specified indicators of achievement
- Started assumptions/remarks.

EXAMPLE

VISION: Improved Standard of Living Goal: Healthy Community by 2024

Objectives	Activities	By Whom	Where	When	Resources Required	Budget KES.	Indicators Of Achievement	Constraints	Remarks
i) Provide clean drinking water to 200 families by 2030	Create awareness on health issues and waterborne diseases	NGOs, CBOs GOK Field workers	Manyani county	December 2024	Human resources with technical expertise	50 million	Enlightened community on health issues and water borne disease. Clean water provided to community	Political interference corruption	Strive to win political goodwill and cooperation from the community
	Identify and train community health workers	NGOs, CBOs GOK Field workers		January 2023	Human resource, training materials	20 million	Competent trained health workers	Timely availability of funds	
	Mobilize community to dig boreholes	Field workers		March 2023	Skilled labour and implements for digging bore holes	30 million	Number of bore holes dug	Availability of skilled workers	
	Train community water committee on borehole protection and maintenance	Contractors Field workers		November 2024		10 million	Number of functional boreholes, well protected and maintained	Cooperation for the beneficiaries	
ii) to reduce infant mortality by 10% by 2024	Create awareness on importance of child immunization	Trained community health workers	Manyani county	March 2024	Immunization and other essential drugs	10 million	Number of immunized children	Availability of funds	Seek assistance form Government and development partners
	Initiate progress and child development programs								

MODULE 5
PROJECT PLANNING ND MANAGEMENT

Luke 14. 28-30 (NKJV) "For which of you intending to build a tower, does not sit down first and. count the cost, whether he has enough to finish it lest after he has laid the foundation is not able to finish. All who shall see it begin to mock him, saying this man began to build and he is not able to finish.

1 Chronicle 22. 14 17 NKJV - "Indeed I have taken much trouble to prepare for the house of the LORD, one hundred thousand talents of gold, and one million talents of silver; and bronze and iron beyond measure, for it is so abundant. I have prepared timber and stone also and you may add to them Moreover there are with you in abundance: woodmen and stonecutters, and all types of skillful men for every kind of work. Of gold and silver and bronze and iron there is no limit. Arise and begin working, and the LORD be with you. David also commanded all leaders of Israel to help his son Solomon to build the temple so they bring back the ARK of the Covenant of the Lord and holy articles of God into the house that is to be built for the name of the Lord."

5.1 Introduction

This module explains how to translate development community action plans (vision, goals objectives and activities) into implementable projects to address community needs /problems for sustainable development.

5.2 Objectives

At the end of the module, the participants will be better able to:

1. Define the term project.
2. Describe stages of project development
3. Make a diagrammatic presentation of the project cycle.

4. Explain what is involved in feasibility study (project preparation)
5. Describe project appraisal and final approval stage.
6. Explain project implementation and management.
7. Explain project monitoring and evaluation.

5.3 Definition of A Project

The term project can be explained in many different ways as.

1 A project is an activity that uses both human and non-human resources to achieve specific purposes.
2 Projects are building blocks of development.
3 A project has a definite start time, definite completion time and is defined within specific limits in terms of resources, time, scope and space.
4 Projects use specific inputs (resources)to produce particular set outputs over specified time period in order to meet identified development needs/problems (e.g., provision of health facility) of clearly defined target groups.
5 Projects use scarce resources to achieve objectives that are expected to bring change for the target group.

Projects require a special approach that involves resource mobilization, coordination, organization, collaboration, integration and effective monitoring and evaluation to ensure that implementation is carried out according to the project plan. Effective project planning and management is needed to ensure that project objectives are achieved.

5.4 Stages of Project Development

A development project matures through distinct stages in its life cycle which extends from identification of community needs /problems to conversion into routine operations of the project.

The different stages of project development are:

1. Project planning stage
   - Project identification
   - Project preparation (feasibility study)
   - Project appraisal and selection /approval.
2. Implementation and management stage
   - Project implementation
   - Project monitoring and evaluation
   - Output generation and distribution.
3. Operations stage
   - It involves actual production and distribution of output, as the project is realized.

The relationship between the stages of a project are as shown below

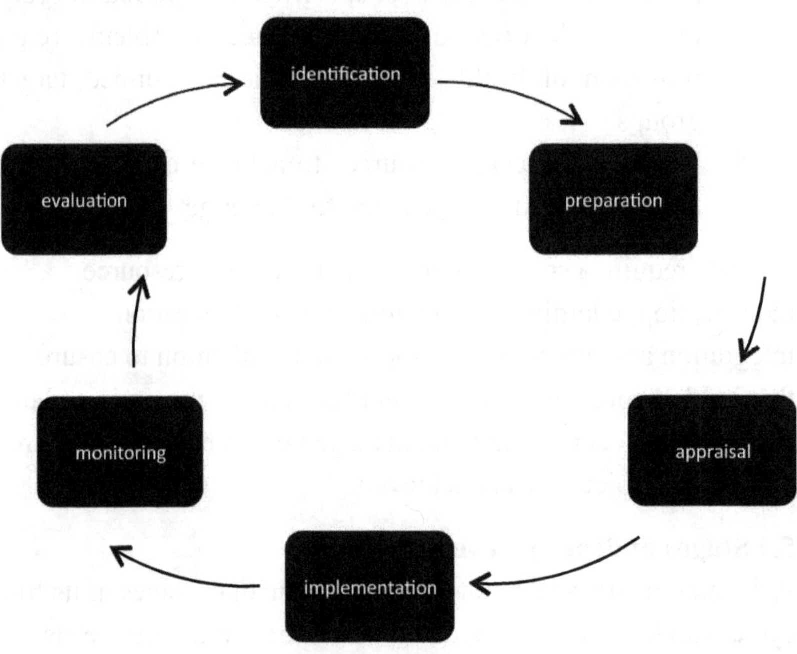

5.4 Project Planning Stage

This stage includes:

(a) Project Identification

This is done at the community situation analysis stage to identify community needs, problems or opportunities and rank them according to priority and be organized into action plans (CAPS) from which would flow desired project ideas to be implemented.

(b) Project Preparation (feasibility study)

A project feasibility study analyses project aspects listed below to determine factors that will influence successful implementation of the project.

(i) Technical aspects

- Concerned with the project inputs and outputs-materials and the outcome of the project.
- Where the project will be located – is the location of the project suitable
- The environmental impact of the project. How will the project affect the environment?

(ii) Institutional/Organizational/Managerial Aspects

- Institutions responsible for the project implementation and whether they have capacity, both technical and administrative
- Whether the institution has the capacity to manage the project to successful completion.

(iii) Social/Cultural Aspects

- Concerned with the social implication of the project the community.
- whether the project is responsive to the socio/cultural practices of the community.

(iv) Commercial aspects

- Concerned with availability of inputs and market for the outputs.
- Consider the quality and quantity of output in relation to the available market.
- Consider procurement of equipment and supplies to avoid undue delay which would lead to price escalations.

(v) Financial aspects

- considers the financial implication of the project to all parties involved in the project.
- ensures the project gets proper financial backing.
- Ensures proper funding of the project.

(vi) Economic aspects

This helps to determine whether the project is likely to contribute significantly to the development of the community and total economy and whether these contributions significantly justify the use of scarce resources needed by the project.

Also look at the cost benefit compensation. What are the expected economic and social benefits associated with the project and will they exceed its investment and operation costs?

(vii) Project schedule of work

A Gantt chart is useful in scheduling/planning. It is a graphic presentation of activities in a project and the time taken to be implemented. The length of the bar in the chart indicates the total time planned for each task. For example, in the diagram below, time taken foe each activity is shown as follows:

- Activities -1,2 month of January
- Activity 3 month of January and February
- Activities 4,5 month of March to April
- Activity 6 month of May - December
- Activity 7 months from September to December

The Gantt chart is useful in monitoring and reporting on the progress of implementation of project activities.

Gantt chart

ACTIVITY	MONTHS											
7												
6												
5												
4												
3												
2												
1												
	Jan	Feb	Mar	Apr	May	Jun	Jul	Aug	Sep	Oct	Nov	Dec

(viii) The logical framework matrix

The logical framework matrix is a tool used to organize information in order to highlight relations between the appraisal stage and the implementation stage.

For example, Logical Framework Matrix Water Project
Project Goal: Healthy Community by 2015

Project Goal. Healthy community by 2024				
Description	**Objectively verifiable indicators**	**Indicators of achievements**	**Means of verification**	**Assumption/risks**
Objective Purpose To provide clean drinking water to 200 families in Manyani county by 2024, at least 10 families per borehole	-Number of boreholes dug -Number of families accessing clean water	Every targeted has access to water	-Presence of borehole -Project reports	Commitment of community political good will corruption, insecurity
Outcomes -Reduced walking distance for water - Accessibility of clean water to families.	- Number of families' access to clean water - Availability of water to 200 families	Access to clean water reduced to at less than 1 km	-Observation Project reports -Community reports	
Impact -time released for other production work. -reduced water borne diseases -health community	-Time spent fetching water -Incidences of water borne diseases	Reduced time to access clean water Reduced incidences of waterborne disease	Observation Morbidity and mortality rates from water borne diseases	
Activities -sensitize community -dig boreholes -train community on borehole maintenance -handover borehole to community for use and maintenance.	-Number of families sensitized -Number of boreholes dug -Number of families trained on borehole protection and maintenance	Functional and well protected and maintained boreholes	Observation Project reports Reports from beneficiaries	

5.5 Project Appraisal

Project appraisal is a review of the preparation stage, of the various aspects of the planned activities to ensure that the assumptions made about the project are realistic. The concern is whether the project meets the necessary conditions for it to proceed or whether it is the best means to reach set objectives. Project appraisal ensures that scarce resources are being put into investments with the highest returns. Therefore, it scrutinizes in detail the following aspects: -

(i) Technical

Will the project work the way it is proposed?

- Is the location right?
- Is the technology appropriate to community needs and capabilities?

(ii) Financial

- Have financial requirements been worked out properly and their sources identified?
- What is the highest expected return from every shilling invented in the project?

(iii) Commercial

- Is there a market for the project output?
- Will it be sustainable?
- Are there any constraints in getting project inputs?

(iv) Economic

- Does the project contribute sustainably to the overall development of the community and nation?

(v) Social

- How will the community benefit from the project?
- Does it increase their earning capacity?
- Does it make the community independent?
- Will the community be able to sustain the project without external help?

(vi) Managerial

- Does the community have the required capacity to implement the project?
- Will the community be able to manage the project on their own?

(vii) Organizational

- Is the project organized in a manner that allows decisions to be made properly and promptly?

5.6 Project Implementation Stages

Project implementation is a critical phase where most of the resources committed to a project are utilized, and the anticipated benefits realized.

Proper management of this phase ensures timely completion and utilization of the project. Efficient and timely implementation of a project depends on having an implementation plan, project management supervision personnel and timely availability of materials.

(i) Project Implementation Plan – this involves
Implementation planning includes:

- Definition of task to be carried out
- Developing work plans for the entire implementation of the project.
- Scheduling of project activities which specify in detail when/how each activity is to be done, who will manage them and what resources are required.

(ii) Project Execution

Once arrangements for acquiring project resources are finalized, the execution of the project can begin. This outlines who is doing what and to whom.

(iii) Progress Monitoring

This deals with the ongoing assessment of the progress and performance against plans and budget:

- It's concerned with whether the project is being implemented according to the plan.
- Whether project supervision and control is taking place with rapid feedback isolating the possible problems and bottle necks.

(iv) Project Control

This involves choosing milestone indicators for project performance e.g.

- Gathering and analyzing information on project performance in relation to planned activities.
- Establishing procedures for corrective actions when deviations from original plans occur.

The elements that need to be controlled include:

- Accountability for maintenance of time and schedules for the duration of the project.
- Financial performance in terms of allocation and expenditure.
- Project assets such as facilities, machinery and other capital items at the disposal of the project to ensure optimum allocation and utilization.

5.7 Project Completion and Stat-Up Operations

This marks the end of investment period and the beginning of operations.by now all activities of the project have been completed and output is being generated.it marks the end of project implementation status.

The project is handed over to the community for operation and maintenance to provide the goods and services as intended to the project beneficiaries.
Monitoring and evaluation are tools for measuring the progress of a project as it matures from one stage to the next.

5.8 Project Monitoring and Evaluation

Case study: Extension of classroom at Tumaini primary school

The headmaster of Tumaini primary early last year announced the need to construct an additional classroom. In response, the chairperson of the Teachers' Parents' Association immediately mobilized the community and started making bricks by their own efforts. The community members were highly motivated to hear that Saidia NGO offered to roof the classroom for them. They worked diligently to make over 50,000 bricks needed for construction. The parents proceeded to burn the bricks and, in the meantime, hired local builders to start the foundation soon after, they began working on the walls.

The community composed mainly of women who had labored for four weeks in collecting sand and water, breathed a sigh of relief when eventually the wall had risen to wall-plate level. In anticipation they waited for Saidia to bring roofing materials as per their promise. There was a delay for several weeks after which Saidia was sent a reminder of their promised intervention. As usual their technical representative Mr. Wasi, a field officer attached to the region paid a visit to the construction site so as to approve the work done for roofing.

Arriving at the site, Mr. Wasi was shocked by the cracks that had developed on the wall and was therefore dissatisfied with the workmanship. In fact, he was quite furious with the builders. That same afternoon unexpected heavy rains occurred causing the construction walls to collapse. The community was left in a dilemma and very demoralized.

Discussion

1. Discuss what would have saved the situation.
2. What lessons are learnt?
3. What could have been done better?

5.8.1. Monitoring

Monitoring is a continuous function that involves day- to- day, step by step, routine checking. Following project inputs and outputs during project implementation with a view to indicating as early as possible any shortcoming, in order to undertake corrective measures on time.

(i) Reasons for monitoring

- To record accurate information on individual projects
- To provide information for decision making
- To provide information for coordination
- To provide continuous progress reports and reviews
- To document information for evaluating the project at a later stage.

(ii) How monitoring is done

Monitoring is done by collecting and recording information (data) in the form of

- Numbers
- Quantities
- Categories e.g., Number of people
- Amount of group contribution
- Expenditure
- Percentage of work done.

(iii) Project Progress on Monitoring

The main contents of a project progress report are:

- Name of the project
- Project goals and objectives
- Tasks/activities. Resources used.
- Achievements/ progress

- Constraints/problems/shortcomings
- Evaluator's remarks/views/conclusions
- Suggestions/recommendations.

5.8.2. Project Evaluation

Project evaluation is a continuous function with assessing relative measurements of the attainment of goals and objectivities and their impacts on project beneficiaries according to set standards.

(i) Types of evaluations

There are three main types of evaluations

- Ex-ante/pre-project evaluation – is carried out before project implementation to determine the feasibility of a planned project.
- Formative/on-going evaluation –analyses the relationship between inputs, outputs and project outcomes.
- Summative/ex-post/postmortem/final evaluation is performed after complete implementation of the project, attempts to measure progress towards the stated goals and objectives and its impact on the project beneficiaries.

(ii) Reasons for evaluation

- To obtain accurate information on the needs of the target community for planning purposes
- To facilitate decision- making on either changes or adjustments in the project
- To determine the progress made in the project and identify the contributing factors.
- To measure the extent to which the project is meeting its objectives.
- To justify extending of the project if the project is operationally sound.

(iii) Issues to be evaluated

- Project objectives- objectives should be evaluated to determine whether identified community needs are being met.
- Resources (labour, materials machinery, money) whether they are being efficiently being used for the purposes meant for them.
- Personnel performances- whether working professionally and diligently and if they encountered any challenges/problems.

(iv) Evaluators

- Evaluation may be done by internal or external evaluators.
- Internal evaluators are all those involved directly with the project implementation. They have inside information of the project and may be committed to the project.
- External evaluators are usually consultants who come at the end of the project, they may be objective, more thorough but they could be expensive.

(v) Plan for evaluation

- Select topic/aspect/ terms of reference.
- Formulate required questions.
- Consider tools for data collection.
- Collect data.
- Analyze and interpret data.
- Write the report.
- Brief and discuss with concerned parties.

5.8.3. Tools for Monitoring and Evaluation

The main tools for monitoring and evaluation are

(i) The Gantt charts

(ii) The logical framework matrix.

(i) The Gnatt chart

- The Gnatt chart as a monitoring/reporting tool attempts to determine the status of activities carried out and to estimate the percentage of activities completed.
- It can also make an extension or contraction of the duration of the activity.
- The chart provides visual display of activities that are behind or ahead of schedule so that adjustments and reallocation of resources can be made.
- The Gantt chart requires that special explanatory notes be written to explain delayed activities and give reasons behind the delay.
- The chart is especially useful to individuals closely involved in the project.

(ii) Logical framework

- The logical framework matrix helps to:
- State linkages between inputs, outputs, outcomes and impacts.
- Defines project inputs outputs, outcomes and impact in measurable terms.
- Indicators which measure or verify achievements of outputs, outcomes and impacts.
- Clarifies assumptions about the project and measures progress.

MODULE 6

RESOURCE MOBILIZATION

Exodus 12:35-36 (NKJV) - Now the children of Israel had done according to the word of Moses, and they had asked from the Egyptians articles of silver, articles of gold, and clothing. And the LORD had given the people favor in the sight of the Egyptians, so that they granted them what they requested. Thus they plundered the Egyptians.

6.1. Introduction

This module explains how to source for funds for planned projects.

6.2. Objectives

At the end of the module the participants will be able to:

1. Identify different sources of funds for implementation of projects.
2. Explain what a project proposal is.
3. Outline components of a project proposal
4. Write a project proposal for a community.

Case study: Expansion of Mwamba Water Project

Although Mwamba water project was a success story, the members were not satisfied with drawing water from the communal taps. This was still time consuming and tasking especially for the older members of the community. It was an expressed need to expand the water project so that each member could have a water tap at the doorsteps.

The community leader Mr. Lengo convened a meeting for all community members to discuss the issue and plan the way forward. It was resolved that the project be expanded according to the members' wishes. Members quickly contributed funds for project implementation, but only a quarter of the required funds was raised.

The Executive Committee resolved to approach development Partners to assist them raise the short fall of the required funds. The Development Partners advised them to submit a project proposal so that it could be considered alongside other project proposals. They promptly wrote the proposal and submitted it to three development partners. After two weeks, the Chairperson received regrets from all three development partners, with a note that the proposal was not approved by the appraisal committee because it did not measure to their standard. Determined to improve on their proposal. They approached Mr. Fikis, a staff from a local NGO to help them write the proposal. Mr. Fikis agreed to write the proposal at a of 50,000 shillings. With fifty percent down payment. The Executive Committee are still deliberating on how to raise the money.

Discussion

What is your experience of writing a project proposal?

6.3. Sources of Project funding

Funds for community projects can be sourced from the following avenues

- Community members' contribution
- Community institutions contribution
- Non-governmental organizations
- Donor organizations
- Government programs
- Banks
- Private sector a social responsibility
- Savings and credit societies
- Family and friends' contributions
- Others.

6.4. Definition of a Project Proposal

A project proposal is a document presented to funding agencies requesting funds for implementation of specific planned activities to achieve stated objectives and goals. The document describes the community's vision, goals, objectives and activities and strategies on how to achieve them.

6.5. Components of a Project Proposal

Components of a project proposal include:

(i) Summary – Should be about one page.

- It is usually written last, giving a summary of what the proposal is about.

(ii) Introduction - Describes the history of the proposed project and the rationale of the document. It includes:

- References to relevant policies and programmes –
- Relevant demographic information
- Social economic factors
- Persons, groups, agencies relevant to the proposed project
- Relevant literature or statistics

(iii) Background – This provides information about the community group presenting the proposal. The information includes:

- Legal status of the group
- Organizational and management structure of the group
- The group's vision, mission, goals and objectives
- Current activities and achievements
- Planned future activities.
- Current challenges experienced by the group.

(iv) Problem Statement and Justification

This provides brief but comprehensive information on:

- The community problem or need.
- The magnitude of the problem
- The population affected by the problem.
- Projections on the effects of the problem
- The causes of the problem
- Proposed interventions and strategies on how to solve/address the stated problem.

(v) Project Goals and Objectives

This section states the community's ultimate goals and specific objectives. It also outlines specific activities for realization of each objective.

(vi) Implementation Methodology

The section explains how the objectives will be achieved through proposed activities. It also explains the role of stakeholder collaboration and networking. It summarizes activities to be implemented on the Gnatt chart.

(vii) Expected Project Output

This section highlights the expected outcomes from the project activities and its effects on the community.

(viii) Project Monitoring and Evaluation

This section explains how the project will be monitored and evaluated, at what stages, by whom and when. It explains specific reports to be submitted to the relevant parties and by whom.

(ix) Project Sustainability and Community Contribution

This section explains the project's long-term future once it has been completed and after external funding and technical support is phased out. It also explains the role of community in sustaining the project.

(x) Logical Framework

This provides a summary of project design in a matrix in terms of the project aspects listed below-

- Overall goal – vision
- Project purpose
- Specific objectives
- Major activities
- Expected outputs
- Monitoring indicators
- Risks and assumptions.

(xi) Project Budget

This includes the estimated cost of the project, broken down in separate budget lines per year for each objectives and activities to reflect the cost of: -

- Materials
- Equipment
- Personnel
- Training and capacity building
- Constraints
- Transport
- Travel and accommodation allowances
- Administration costs
- Miscellaneous and contingency costs.

(xii) Top Cover Page to show

- Name of applying organization
- Contact address
- Name of project
- Name of the contact/applying officer
- Contact address and email address.

7 CONCLUSION

It is often urged that communities especially from the developing world are poorer than they were many years back in spite of the much resource allocation for improving their wellbeing. Available information shows that some of the factors contributing to this state of affairs is lack of knowledge and technical knowhow of the people to champion their development agenda and passive participation or non- participation in development matters that affect their wellbeing.

However, people themselves can bring about their desired difference in life if they can mobilize and organize themselves in development groups under visionary leadership and taking into consideration gender and governance issues. There are many cases of ghost projects or white elephants that are meant to serve communities to improve their lives.

This manual provides an opportunity for capacity building, especially at community level in the areas of project feasibility study and project cycle development and management. Many a time communities identify and prioritize their development needs, but lack of funds has been a major impediment in achieving their goals.

The module on resource mobilization is aimed at building capacity at community level to source for funds from development partners including the private sector.

This manual is about showing people how to fish instead of them waiting to be brought fish. It is about living with people working with them until they can confidently say, this difference you see in our lives, we did it ourselves and we are proud.

8. REFERENCES

Annette, H. and S. B. Rifkin (1995). Guidelines for Rapid Participatory Appraisals to Assess Community Health Needs. Geneva: WHO/SHS/DHS/95.8.

Aubel, J. (1993). Participatory Program Evaluation. Baltimore: catholic Relief Services and Child Survival Technical Support/USAID.

Bhatnagar, B and A. C. Williams (1992), "Participatory Development and the World Bank. Potential Directions for Change" The World Bank Discussion Papers, No. 183.

Catholic Relief Services. (1999). Rapid Rural Appraisal (RRA) and Participatory Rural Appraisal (PRA). A manual for CRS Field Workers and Partners.

Chambers, R. (1992, October). Rural Appraisal: Rapid, Relaxed and Participatory. Sussex, UK: Institute of Development Studies, discussion paper 311.

Chambers, R. (1997). Who's, Reality counts? London: ITDG. Conflict Research Consortium. Boulder, CO: University of Colorado.

De Negri, B, E. Thomas, A. Ilinigummugabo, I. Muvandi, and Lewis. (1998). Empowering Communities: Participatory techniques for Community Based Programme Development, vol.1(2): trainers' manual (Participant's Handbook).

Fetterman,d.et al.(eds) (1996). Empowerment Evaluation: Knowledge and Tools for Self-Assessment and Accountability. Thousand Oaks, CA Sage Publications.

Feuerstein, M. (1986) Partners in Evaluation: Evaluating Development and Community Programmes with participants. TALC. London: Macmillan.

Goleman, D (1998)." What makes a leader? "Harvard Business Review, November-December, pp.93-102.

Gosling, l. (1995). Toolkits: A practical guide to assessment, Monitoring, Review, and Evaluation. Save the Children Development Manual No.5. London: save the children/UK.

Hope, A. and S. Timmel. (1986). Training for Transformation – A handbook for Community Workers, vol.1-3. Gweru, Zimbabwe: Mambo Press.

Howard-Grabman, 1 (2000). "Bridging the gap between communities and service providers: Developing accountability through Community Mobilization Approaches. "Institute of Development Studies Bulletin, vol.31(1):88-96.

Huizer, G (1997)." Participatory Action Research and Peoples Participation Introduction and Case Studies." SD Dimensions. Rome Sustainable Development Department, FAO.

Hyma, B., and P. Nyamwange. 1993). Women's role and participation in farm and community tree growing activities in Kiambu District, Kenya.

International Institute of Environment and Development. (1995) A Trainers' Guide for Participatory Learning and Action, London: International institute for environmental and development.

International institute for Environment and Development (1995). Participatory Learning in action notes: London Sustainable Agriculture Programme, International Institute for Environment and Development.

International Institute of Rural Reconstruction. (1998). Participatory Monitoring and Evaluation: Experiences and Lessons. Workshop Proceedings. Siland, Cavite, Philippines: International Institute of Rural reconstruction, James Yen centre.

Leach, (1994). "Building Capacity through Action Learning"
ÏDR Reports, vol.10(5):1-29.

Maddux, R B. (1992) Team Building: An Exercise in Leadership. Los Altos, CA: Crisp Publication.

MAP International (1997) "Community Participation Assessment Tool". Presented at a Community Mobilization Workshop Sponsored By John Hopkins University Center For Communication Programs And Save The Children/US, Cochabamba, Bolivia.

Mulwa F W (2004) Demystifying Participatory community development. Beginning with the people ending with people. Zapf Chancery and P. Olivex publishers.

Oakley, P. (1995). Peoples 'Participation in Development projects. London: INTRAC. Overseas Development Administration. (1995) A Guide to Social Analysis for Projects in Developing Countries. London: HMSO).

Parker, A.R., et al. (1995). Gender Relations Analysis: A Guide for Trainers. Westport, CT: Save The Children/USA.

Parker. and R. Krupp. (1992).50 Activities for Team Building, Vol.1.Amherst, MA: Human Resource Development Press.

Pretty, J., I. Gujit, J. Thompson, and I. Scoones. (1995). Participatory Learning and Action: a Trainers Guide. London: international institute for environment and development.

Schubert,B.et al. (1994). Facilitating the Introduction of a Participatory and Integrated Development Approach (PIDA) In Kilifi District, Kenya. Vol. II (Methods)Berlin: CATAD.

Vella, J K et al. (1995) Training through dialogue. Promoting Effective Learning from our Development Approach.

Wellborn, A, (1994) participatory rural appraisal and needs analysis: whose knowledge counts? Kenya: Proceedings of The International Symposium On Participatory Research in Health Promotion.

The World Bank (1999) "Designing Community Based Development" Environment Development Dissemination Note, Number 17.

And Social Assessment: Tools and Techniques. Washington, DC: The World Bank.

The world bank. (1994). Participatory Development Toolkit: Materials to Facilitate Community Empowerment. Washington, DC: The World Bank.

www.ingramcontent.com/pod-product-compliance
Lightning Source LLC
LaVergne TN
LVHW050315160826
845677LV00014B/3403

* 9 7 8 9 9 1 4 9 9 3 0 0 4 *